A Star Trek™ Catalog

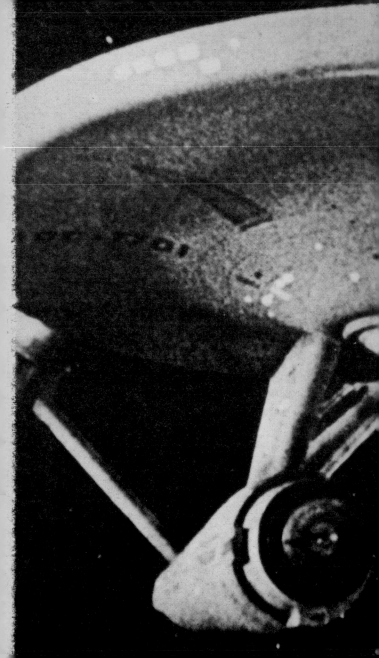

A
Star Trek™
Catalog

Edited by
Gerry Turnbull

Designed by
Nell Appelbaum

Contributors:
Ruth Beck
Jim Burns
Bernadette Lamb
Alex Stern

Special
Guest Star:
Stephen Lewis

Special
Appearance by
Gene Roddenberry

Grosset & Dunlap
Publishers New York
A Filmways Company

To Gene Roddenberry with appreciation
for his talent, foresight and imagination.

**Every effort has been made to explore
the full realm of the universe of *Star
Trek* fans. We are grateful to those many
people who lent their time, talent and
help to this project. In compiling lists of
manufacturers, fan clubs, books, etc.,
we have again tried to be as
comprehensive as possible. However,
omissions do not reflect on a service,
product, or quality, nor does inclusion in
these pages constitute an endorsement
or recommendation.**

A STAR TREK CATALOG
Copyright © 1979 Paramount Pictures
Corporation
All Rights Reserved
ISBN: 0-441-78477-1
Tempo Books is registered in the U.S.
Patent Office
Published simultaneously in Canada
Printed in the United States of America
Book Published by Tempo Books /Grosset
& Dunlap Under License
From Paramount Pictures Corporation,
The Trademark Owner

Contents

Introduction

Trekdom and Its
Fantastic Fans

Beginning just a decade ago, seventy-eight 53-minute shows beamed once a week across the American ether; thus was born the **Star Trek** ᵗᵐ phenomenon.

When the network threatened cancellation after the first two seasons, a deluge of objections from outraged viewers forced the **NBC** executives to reconsider—but only temporarily. Following the 1968–1969 season, a recharged letter campaign proved ineffective; production ceased and **ST** went dark. A disinterested observer might be forgiven for assuming that the starship **Enterprise** had made its final voyage. Another candidate for the mothball fleet.

Not at all. In syndication, the series went on to be shown on 142 stations in the U.S.—usually five times a week— and in more than fifty foreign countries. Since 1969, the last year of network airing, the shows have been seen by more people than had ever heard of them during the initial three seasons. In addition, twenty-two animated episodes began a two-season run in the fall of 1972. They, too, went into syndication, beginning in October of 1976.

But **ST**'s influence ranged far beyond filling up space in the television schedule. For instance, the 134-inch balsa

wood and plastic studio model of the **Enterprise** (pretty much as modified by the Anderson Company, an aeronautic display house, in the spring of 1966) is on display at the National Air and Space Museum in Washington, D.C. In the Rocketry and Space Flight Gallery of the museum (a part of the Smithsonian Institution) short clips of **ST** episodes are continually screened. And NASA's first space shuttle will not make its premiere voyage as the *Constitution,* the original choice; instead, at the 1976 roll-out, the craft was christened the **Enterprise.**

Perhaps most important, however, is the dedication that **ST** fans, numbering in the hundreds of thousands (at least!), have brought to the object of their affection. With more than 200 fan organizations, almost as many fan publications, a full convention calendar (and conventions so thronged that the largest hotels in New York must turn away thousands attempting to attend), the fans are the soul and substance of the **ST** phenomenon.

They have literally forced a movie version out of Holly-wood executives who couldn't see the forest for their laminated plastic bookshelves—and woe to the station man-

ager who decides to replace the syndicated series with reruns of *The Big Valley!* Meanwhile, collectors have made
ST memorabilia big business. For years, the trading of
prized mementos (from the shooting of the episodes and
out-takes to original artwork) was a strictly inter-fan affair.
Within recent years, however, huge manufacturers have
moved into assembly-line production with a wide variety of
merchandise—posters, toys, games, models, the works.
This merchandising is of such magnitude that corporations
have been founded upon **ST** memorabilia, with their profits in the six- and even seven-digit bracket. Some long-
time fans resent this intrusion into the world that they, after
all, are credited for creating.

Yet the spirit of the fans remains untarnished, for their
dedication has nothing to do with commercialism. Let the
kids buy their toy phasers, cells, and crystals, no harm
done. For that matter, even the shows themselves are not
the primary focus. It's the ideas—and ideals—expressed
in the **ST** stories that are the vital factor. The optimistic
vision of a future beyond the stars is still ours to cherish.

An Interview with Gene Roddenberry

by Gerry Turnbull

Gene Roddenberry's background as an airline pilot, schooled in aeronautical engineering, combined with his talent as a writer, made up a perfect balance for the man who was to create the most unique science fiction institution on television. In this interview, granted exclusively for **Star Trek Catalog**, Roddenberry discusses that creation and the phenomenon it became.

GT: How did **Star Trek** originate?

GR: It came out of two things. One, I read science fiction, and have all my life. I'd never seen it on television and rarely in film done the way I thought it should be done . . . with more emphasis on believable characters. It seems that most motion picture attempts before were too sketchy, with the emphasis on gadgets.

And the second reason was that television was very censored at the time. You couldn't talk about new ideas relating to sex, politics, religion, or war. I decided to steal a page out of Jonathan Swift's book, *Gulliver's Travels,* and talk about some strange polka-dotted people and be able to get away with those things which the censors might now overlook.

GT: Who first picked up on the concept when you presented it for television?

GR: It was Desilu. I had presented it around town [Hollywood] and there wasn't much interest. Well, Desilu saw something in it and picked it up. When Desilu sold out to Paramount, this project came with it. Paramount bought Desilu during the second year of production, somewhere around the fiftieth episode. You could say that Paramount actually inherited **Star Trek**.

GT: Mr. Roddenberry, surely *Star Wars, Battlestar Galactica, Close Encounters,* and the like, have achieved a great deal of success, you'll agree. Do you believe that **Star Trek** was the forerunner of their success?

GR: I think that's true and I think that the people responsible for the production of those vehicles did an excellent job with them. I liked *Star Wars* very much. They [the producers] realized it too [that **ST** was the forerunner]. They've never written formal letters of thanks but they know that we set the audience for their vehicles and their successes. In fact, *Star Wars* advertised at our conventions the year prior to its release. They pretty well know where their basic audience was, and the non-science fiction fans who were forced by their sons and daughters home from college were also set up for the aftermath of **Star Trek**.

I wasn't looking for any sense of credit with *Star Wars,* but I thought it might have been nice to have them fish me out so that I wouldn't have had to stand in a three-block-long line to see *Star Wars.*

I hope also that this whole thing leads to a more imaginative form of writing, as I do not view science fiction writing as the more limited and narrow thing that most people in television and motion pictures see. Most people think of it in terms of zap guns and rocket ships and don't see it as the enormously broad area of literature it involves.

They don't realize that they are reading science fiction almost daily anyway.

GT: How do you view the phenomenon, the fan clubs, the fanzines and so on? Do you see it as an offshoot or a propagation of **Star Trek**?

GR: We didn't make it happen. It happened and caused **Star Trek** to rehappen! It was a true fan phenomenon and ABC in those days used to think that in some Machiavellian way I'd created the whole phenomenon and that I was able to pick up my phone and say that I wanted five hundred people picketing Rockefeller Center the following night. I used to try and tell them that if I were capable of doing that I'd get the hell out of show business and get into politics!

As far as my personal feelings go regarding the clubs and zines, I wish them well and I'm delighted when I hear of them helping people in some way—of which there have been numerous instances—though I do try and keep myself separate from that. I'm not a **Star Trek** animal, I'm Gene Roddenberry, private citizen, and I'm interested in a whole world of things other than **Star Trek**.

GT: What projects are you working on at present?

GR: I'm working on a novel now, the novelization of **Star Trek—The Movie**, and working on the film itself. I'm also working on a couple of projects dealing with psychic phenomena, about which I'm conferring with a couple of doctors at Stanford Research Institute. I see them as either film vehicles or television movies dealing with precognition and clairvoyance. They're dealing with these elements at Stanford in rigidly controlled laboratories and it's extremely interesting to follow their work.

GT: What has been your greatest pleasure in **Star Trek**?

GR: Well, my greatest pleasure out of **Star Trek** has been the things it takes me to. For instance, I have here on my desk a letter from Sperry Univac in London inviting me to come over to participate in some conferences and seminars dealing with the new uses of computers in the future. And in April I'll receive the Freedom Through Information

Award in Washington, which has previously gone to such luminaries as Bob Hope. These are the real rewards to me of **Star Trek**, and they're a lot of fun also.

GT: With regard to production drawbacks, costuming, makeup, studio shots, and special effects, can you recall a particular problem?

GR: There was one special drawback and that was in the shooting schedule. We had six days within which to shoot each series [episode] and that is the equivalent of half a science fiction motion picture—shot in six days! The sheer pressure of time was something! All those ideas to come up with—new ones each week—and a full script with dialogue. Like most television writers, I'm very content to do three or four scripts a year and here we were doing one a week.

I had a marvelous group of people to work with, not only here in the office but a top notch crew also. When I realized what a tough job I had ahead of me, I hired young people whom I raised to head a particular department, and I figured [that] here was their chance to prove themselves and that they would work hard to accomplish our mutual goals. I was also blessed with fine actors who could handle last-minute rewrites and memorize lines in a blink. The show wasn't a Gene Roddenberry event, it was a real group co-operative effort. The credit I will take is for bringing those people together, but I can't take credit for their wit, talent and ingenious timing.

With regard to the makeup, Leonard had some initial misgivings about the ears, but that passed. The time element for the makeup application meant that he had to show up for makeup a couple of hours before we started shooting each morning.

GT: What was your role in relation to the animated version?

GR: Well, Dorothy Fontana, who had worked with me on the series, oversaw the animated version and I acted as consultant for the project. The budget was such that it couldn't afford a large overhead. She was billed as story editor, but in effect ran the show and I gave advice. The animated version set the way for the young viewers that would later watch the [live-action] series. By its nature, the animated version is stuck in the Saturday morning slot though the people who did it did it very well.

GT: Surely you'd hoped for success with **Star Trek**, but had you foreseen the magnitude of it at any time?

GR: No, I'd hoped that over the years someone might say they'd seen it and liked it, maybe even found it pleasant. I thought that we were rather unique in our concept in that we were basically a non-violent show and we talked about affection for things and other life forms . . . we talked about very positive philosophies, tolerance, and understanding. I thought a few people might like it, but I never expected the phenomenon.

Gene Roddenberry, the creative genius behind ST, graciously autographs his fans' programs at the Cons. Sharon Olson, Kandy Barber, and Kaye Schuchman gleefully await their turn. Photo courtesy of John S. Fong, UFP of Phoenix.

The Cons

Introduction

The conventions have played a critical role in the development of **ST** fandom. For members of the outside world, the big media splash the early conventions made was often their first news of the phenomenon. And, in addition to the obvious functions the
cons provide—seeing and hearing the **ST** personnel
in the flesh, film screenings, general good fellowship
—it's the only time some of the larger fan organizations can get all their members under one roof! Atten-
dance at cons has snowballed: from a few thousand
visitors in 1972, the New York City **Star Trek** con
grew to 15,000 by 1974—and several thousand
more had to be turned away at the door. The 1975
New York City con offered a star-studded guest list
that included Gene Roddenberry, William Shatner,
George Takei, Majel Barrett, and Robert Lansing
(star of the "Assignment Earth" episode). Less public
figures like Isaac Asimov, talented **ST** set designer
Bill Theiss, and writer David Gerrold ("The Trouble
with Tribbles") also participated in panel discussions

or just mingled among the exhibits and fans. Screenings included six **ST** episodes and—a rare treat—Gene Roddenberry's own print (black and white, unfortunately) of the original, unshown pilot, "The Cage."

Conventions are by no means confined to the "Big Apple": those just tend to draw larger crowds and, since most major news organizations are based in New York, receive heavier publicity and promotion. All across the country (and the world) cons large and small are held constantly—some restricting their scope to **ST**, others including the entire range of S–F and sometimes comics as well. The early Equicon on the West Coast rivals anything New York has to offer. The March 1976 con featured, in addition to such **ST** personalities as Roddenberry and Barrett, the great S–F film master George Pal. Bjo Trimble, who began the letter-writing campaign that saved **ST** for the 1968–1969 season, and her husband John organize the annual Equicon.

Our Man Goes to a Convention

(Our Man: novelist Stephen Lewis)

Stardate: 7609.03–7609.06
The Mission: To explore Bicentennial 10, the ST convention at New York's Statler Hilton Hotel and communicate with other "life forms". . . .

As the cab skidded and careened in the direction of the Statler Hilton (the driver had decided to get into the spirit of things by traveling at warp 7) I wondered if, perhaps, Starfleet Command hadn't made a mistake. It wasn't that I didn't like **Star Trek**. Like millions of Americans, I watch the reruns religiously. Along with *I Love Lucy*, **ST** is one of those rare television programs that is even more enjoyable once you've become familiar with most of the episodes.

But space? The final frontier? It's not exactly my sphere of expertise. In truth, I'm more familiar with the Bay City setting of *Another World* than I am with the galaxies traveled by Captain Kirk and his crew—and I couldn't help thinking that I'd be more comfortable sitting in Ada McGowan's kitchen talking about Rachel's marital problems than I'd be at the Statler, trying to bluff my way

Left:
DeForest Kelley is shown addressing the audience at a Con held in Kansas City in 1976. Photo courtesy of Ann C. Teipen.

Right:
Nichelle Nichols and Grace Lee Whitney at the 1976 New York Con. Photo: Maje Waldo.

through some chit-chat about the blueprints and floorplans (or whatever they call them) of the USS **Enterprise**.

Earlier in the week I'd called the official phone number and heard a taped message from George Takei telling me where, when, and how much. I was going to Bicentennial 10 as an assignment, but there were other people—thousands of them—who were going for the fun of it. As I got out of the cab, I catalogued an assortment of "creatures" I expected to meet.

Children and Trekkies (the media's term for the devout **ST** fan) shooting their fake phasers at people as they spoke back and forth on their communicators . . . balding ultra-scientific types, with pocket calculators or slide rules handy, ready to figure a trajectory at the drop of a coordinate . . . screaming, screeching fans eager to paw William Shatner, George Takei, DeForest Kelley, Walter Koenig, James Doohan, Grace Lee Whitney, or Nichelle Nichols, the stars who were to attend . . . and, of course, little old blue-haired ladies in tennis shoes.

I couldn't have been more wrong.

ST's most devoted fans—and some of those at Bicentennial 10 were so devoted that they'd traveled hundreds, even thousands of miles to attend—are actually quite *nice*. As conventions go, the crowd at this one was a lot more pleasant and better behaved than the Democrats (no "Dump the Hump" signs) or the Republicans. They are not, as one who is in on a press pass might first assume, an assortment of misfits who prefer the fantasies of Gene Roddenberry to their own lives, but rather a friendly, outgoing, and articulate cross section of people—the very kind of people one would like to think of as being representative of America.

On the escalator that led to the mezzanine of the hotel, where most of the action started, I struck up a conversation with the McNally family of Des Moines, Iowa. Husband, wife, and two sons, ages thirteen and nine, they looked like the typical family you see on TV commercials, the sort of healthy-looking group that smiles at you from its annual Christmas card. Somehow it was easier to imagine Frank McNally at the office and Betty in the kitchen or on the tennis court than it was to realize that they'd been transported to Bicentennial 10, but there they were.

"My friends think it's ridiculous," Betty McNally confided, "but I think it's terrific! The boys saved their money from their allowances and doing odd jobs. That was what got me interested in the show. I wanted to see why my children were motivated to save money."

Betty began to watch **ST** in syndication.

"At first I thought, 'Oh, God, it's a monster series,' " she recalls. "Tommy, my oldest boy, told me to pay attention, and I did. After a few episodes, I was totally involved. More than that, though, I was glad that my sons were watching it. The show was a kind of model for them, and I realized that they liked the spooky-looking aliens and the technical effects, but what turned them on most of all was the idea of the **Enterprise**, the idea of different kinds of people working together, accomplishing something for the good of the world.

"It was an idea that Frank and I had tried to get across to the boys, but we'd had problems. I think we came across as sounding old-fashioned. The boys would listen

Kathy Betterton puts the finishing touches on her portrait of DeForest Kelley at the 1976 New York Con. Photo: UPI.

"I think I've got them all?" Photo: Maje Waldo.

Hail, Hail, the gang's all here! From left to right, Fred Phillips, the extraordinarily talented makeup man for the ST series, DeForest Kelley, Nichelle Nichols, Leonard Nimoy, George Takei, and Walter Koenig at a 1974 ST Con. Photo courtesy of New Eye Studios.

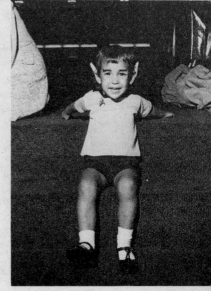

Just resting my ears after a long day at the 1976 Con. Photo: Maje Waldo.

to us, but then they'd read the papers or see the news. Or for that matter, watch the other TV shows. **Star Trek** conveyed a lot of the basic beliefs we wanted our children exposed to, and it did it without any preaching. The boys love the show. I think it's a shame they aren't doing new episodes."

Frank McNally agreed with his wife. He'd been the latecomer of the family, he explained.

"I used to tease Betty when she began to watch the show," Frank told me. "But after a while, I wanted to see what it was about. I have to admit I thought it was a kid show at first. Now? Well, those **Star Trek** episodes are more than just programs for us. For the kids, it's a combination of science class and Sunday school. It's opened their minds to new interests and ideas and you know, it's one of the few things we can really watch and enjoy together as a family."

The McNally's went on their way to explore the various exhibits, and so did I. Having been the kind of boy who always spilled a little glue just when that model of the B-52 was almost assembled, I couldn't help but be impressed by the accomplishment of twenty-three-year-old Michael McMaster of Poughkeepsie, N.Y.: a full-scale, life-size mock-up of the USS **Enterprise**'s bridge, complete with multicolored blinking lights and space-age captain's chair. It was so realistic I expected to see Captain Kirk himself come through the door.

"It cost me about three thousand dollars," Michael told me. He was tired, having just uncrated and reassembled his handiwork. "This is the second one I've built. At first, my parents thought I was crazy. Then they saw it, and they saw what happened at the conventions. . ."

What happened at the conventions was that onlookers thronged to admire Michael's handiwork—and to pay a couple of dollars to sit in the captain's chair and have their picture taken. Michael McMaster strikes me as a young man who could do very well in aerospace—or in television.

Having witnessed this impressive display, I was a little taken aback by the eight-member, self-proclaimed "Grunge" group, made up of boys between the ages of sixteen and eighteen. With their aluminum foil hats and antennae, and those blue circles around their eyes, I wondered if these might not be the "Peck's bad boys" of inner space. It turned out that they were members of a science fiction club from West Islip High School. They'd come in for the day, they explained, and someone they'd met on the train from Long Island has supplied the make-up. Hardly intent on raising any kind of intergalactic hell, they asked me to be sure to say hello to their teacher, Mrs. Kummer. (Hello, Mrs. Kummer, wherever you are. . .)

In the Grand Ball Room and the Gold Ball Room, a series of screenings was going on non-stop. Besides **ST** episodes, science fiction films were shown, ranging from a showing of *The Time Machine,* to the movie premiere of *Universe,* narrated by William Shatner. For the devotee, the twenty-dollar, three-day admission price was a bargain . . . out of this world, one might say.

In the Ivy Suite, the stars of the series—both on-camera personalities and behind-the-scenes creative contributors—lectured and answered questions, often surprisingly technical and intelligent ones, from the audience.

On the mezzanine, display space was at a premium, shared by those who were out to turn the dollars (the owners of licenses to produce and/or sell the phasers, posters, buttons, toys, books, and stills) and the less commercial-minded fan clubs, each displaying their fanzines.

Kathy Bayne, an attractive girl-next-door-looking young woman, founded the American branch of Hosato, a George Takei club, in January of 1976.

"The British club was started in 1974," she informed me. "I've met George, and he's directly involved with the club. To me, a fan club should always be non-profit. Making money for the sake of making money isn't right. I have

Leonard Nimoy and
Arlene Martel entering
the Chicago ST Con in
1975. Photo courtesy of
New Eye Studio.

A loyal fan, Albert Licata,
scans the array of photos
for one he doesn't already
have. Photo: UPI.

Above:
It's all smiles for the crowd at the 1974 New York Con. Photo: New Eye Studios.

Center:
This gleeful group trekked all the way from Long Island for the 1976 New York Con. Photo: Maje Waldo.

Bottom:
The always busy personnel at the booths take a short break between T-shirt sales. Photo: Maje Waldo.

a job working for the airlines. It's nice, because I get to go to a lot of the conventions.

"**Star Trek** is a hobby for me. I have all the books and some of the posters. I like the idea of everyone getting along. It's a nice way to meet people. I've made some wonderful friends by attending conventions like this one."

How does a mother react when her daughter starts a fan club for a supporting player of a series that's been off the air, in terms of active production, for a number of years?

"I think it's just great!" Polly Bayne, Kathy's mother, told me, smiling and obviously enjoying herself. "Some of my friends think it's a little strange that I'm involved, but a lot of them like the show. It appeals to people of all ages. As far as the club goes, it's run out of our home in Woodside, New York. I'm the treasurer," she added, with a wink. "I'm very good at numbers. We started with a hundred members, but it's grown to almost twice that so far."

Mary Ellen Goodwin's heart is invested in the Nichelle Nichols fan club in Ayer, Massachusetts. She's been involved for three years, is divorced, and is the mother of two sons, eleven and thirteen, and a six-year-old daughter.

"I like the idea behind the series," she said. "The idea of people getting together, being themselves but still working to solve problems. I especially like Nichelle. She's a very talented actress and a beautiful person. Our club is called Furaha."

Jan Boll is a twenty-four-year-old factory worker who is active in the Star Trek Club at Michigan State University. "My folks can't stand it," she readily admits, "and some of my friends merely tolerate my interest in **Star Trek**. But for every one who's neutral, I have another who loves it. I have ten pen pals whom I write to regularly that I met through the conventions. I got into it because I liked the show, and because it's nice to get into something that lets you share a common interest with other people."

Walking around at Bicentennial 10, it was impossible not to be struck by a sense of camaraderie. Everyone I met was pleasant. People struck up conversations or renewed acquaintances from other conventions with a naturalness and ease that is rare in our society. If someone bumped into you in a rush to get to one of the numerous screenings or autograph sessions, most of the time they actually stopped and said, "Excuse me—."

From people of all ages and backgrounds, the responses were the same. The conventions are important to them as a link to something that is important to their lives. **ST** is more than a TV show; it is an *ideal,* or rather a series of images showing an almost universal ideal in action.

"What I came here for," Billy Casslin, a college student from Atlanta, Georgia, told me, "was to confirm the fact that there are thousands of people who feel the same as I. I always wanted to come to New York but felt that I would feel out of place. The convention gave me the perfect combination. My girlfriend, who is also a big fan of the series, came with me.

"We'll be out sometimes and I can say something to her that we both understand because of the show. It's a private way of communicating. And after a full day of classes, after you listen to the news and see how lousy things are going, you can turn on the TV and watch **Star Trek** and escape for a while."

ST is extremely popular on college campuses. At Harvard, where the wall-size TV screen was developed, it was a favorite with those who watched technological history in the making.

The premium floor space was taken up by the major retailers, among them Langley Associates, a Michigan-based corporation that includes three partners, five full-time employees, and occasional extra help as needed. For Nancy Perri's husband and his associates, **ST** has become a big mail-order business.

"The company started," Nancy told me as we stood amid the displays of buttons, posters, and stills, "as fans with an idea—making buttons. When my husband and I went to our first convention in December, 1972, I was apprehensive. I didn't think that the buttons would go. We had two hundred of them, and before we could even get the display unit assembled, they were being snatched out of our hands. Next came the posters, then the eight-by-ten stills and slides. I'm really amazed by the entire thing."

ST, make no mistake, is big business—and a lot of that business is done at conventions like Bicentennial 10. From Spock ears to phasers, from scripts of the show (which are very expensive collector's items) to stills, the cash-merchandise exchange went at a fast clip.

One man who sells **ST** merchandise asked not to be identified, but was willing to share his candid comments on the merchandising of **ST**.

"Me, I've been in mail order all my life. Elvis, I sold. Beatles, Monkees, I sold. But I never saw anything like this. Most things, you know, they come and they go—the trend passes, people change, they want something new. Take your Davy Crockett hats and your hula hoops . . . big, right? But not for long.

"This **Star Trek** is a different animal. The show is off the air, but you'd never know it. New people—all ages, too—get interested in it when they see it in syndication. Right away they want the books, the records, the buttons, the posters. I think everyone would agree that business is better now than it was when the show was on the network. The cult is building, building, building. . ."

"Has the cult peaked now?" I asked.

"What? Are you kidding me?" the man answered. "Look here, right here. Tonight there's a Spock Look-alike Contest. Tomorrow, there's the big ball. It's sold out, been sold out for weeks, did you know that?"

I had to admit I didn't.

"And next year, just you wait!" he said, gleefully. "Next year when the movie version gets made, business is going to be better than ever. I wouldn't even be surprised if the fans get the network to put the show back on again, to make new episodes."

Whether they succeed or not is almost academic. At this point, the fans of **ST**, their numbers ever increasing, seem quite content to enjoy the old episodes, to laugh at a well-worn "blooper" reel of out-takes from the series, to collect their fanzines and buttons and posters . . . occasionally even to dress up in costumes representing their favorite **ST** characters.

Once in a while, as they did at Bicentennial 10, they like to get together to share something that is important to them —and they manage to do it with a degree of friendliness, pleasantness, and good-natured wholesomeness that is very refreshing. It's nice to see families doing things together without either parents or children looking bored. It is moving to see a young boy in a wheel chair, dressed in a USS **Enterprlse** uniform, smiling as he zaps a friend with a toy phaser. It's nice to see people having a good time, not because they've been told they should (Smile—you're in Disneyland!) but because they are really enjoying themselves.

When's the next convention? I think I'll go.

Stephen Lewis, author of Something in the Blood, The Best Sellers, *and the forthcoming* Fear No Evil, *now feels he "never knew from* Star Trek" *prior to this assignment. Furthermore, he claims to have found the perfect excuse for avoiding literary cocktail parties: "I have to catch my shows!"*

Bill Shatner never seems to tire of answering questions from the audience. For his wit and charm he is a welcome guest at any Con. Photo courtesy of the United Friends of Wil-liam Shatner, Ann C. Telpen, photographer.

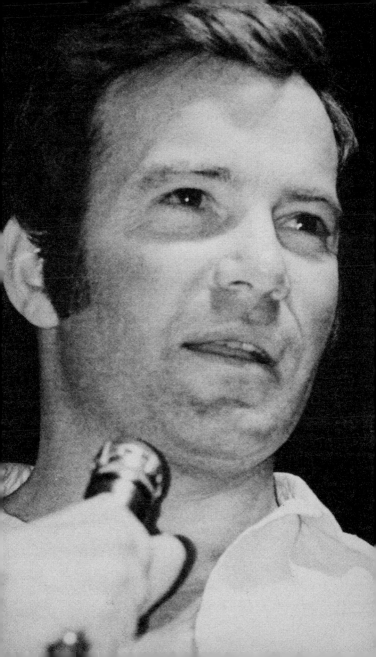

The Clubs
and
Organizations

In our book, and in any Trekker's, the Star Trek Welcomittee is first and foremost in fandom's organizations. This non-profit group works through 150 volunteers in thirty-five states and four countries. Their mission: to provide an "umbrella" for all Trekfans—their organizations and activities; to answer, free of charge, questions about **Trek** technology, episodes, actors, trivia, revivals, fans in your area, starting a club or zine or newsletter. They ask only that you send a self-addressed, stamped envelope (SAS envelope) with your inquiry to: ST Welcommittee, P. O. Box 207, Saranac MI 48881.

Their **Directory of Star Trek Organizations** (updated every few months) lists clubs, zines, books, sales items, cons—another great service. Send $1 to STW Directory, Allyson Whitfield, P. O. Box 206, New Rochelle, New York 10804. There's a wealth of info as well in **A Piece of the Action** (APOTA), the Welcommittee's monthly report on **Trek** and fandom news; it also has occasional feature articles. The price is $5.50 a year, $2.75 half a year. Write STW Monthly Report, Kathe Donnelly /Karolyn Popovich,

P. O. Box 19413, Denver, Colorado 80219. The booklet **So You Want Publicity** tells how to publicize clubs, zines, cons. Send $1 plus 15¢ stamp to: A. Boyer, 2086 Cunningham, Warren, Michigan 48091. Checks must be made to A. Boyer. Will answer specific questions about publicity, if you send a SAS envelope with your letter. If you read **APOTA** regularly, you'll also find fans' interesting, original publicity ideas described. Look for this in the Publicity Department's column.

To defray printing and mailing cost of the Info Service, the Welcommittee raises funds by selling **ST** patches. See the Marketspace section in this book for details.

We acknowledge gratefully the Welcommittee's assistance to us in preparing this section of our book. In particular, we wish to thank STW chairwoman Helen Young and **Directory** editor Allyson Whitfield for their generous cooperation.

Clubs are listed in alphabetical order, based on geographical location. All fees quoted are subject to change. Keep in mind that our listing of a club does not signify an

In a turnabout, Eleen seems to be advising Dr. McCoy in "Friday's Child." Artist: Joni Wagner for Furaha.

Next page:

Dr. McCoy is shown at ease for a moment after the recovery of Captain Kirk who was stricken while on an alien planet. © Paramount Pictures Corporation.

endorsement of it. Although every effort has been made to ensure accuracy, we cannot be responsible for changes in the addresses listed. **Be sure to send a self-addressed, stamped (SAS) envelope with all correspondence to a club.** We have abbreviated addresses and have used **NL** to indicate newsletter.

Alabama

Southern Fandom Confederation, Meade Fierson III, 3705 Woodvale Road, Birmingham, AL 35223

Mobile Area Trekkers Association (MATA) Write: MATA, c/o Chuck Raue, 804 Rowell Street, Mobile, AL 36606

Arizona

Star Trek Intermountain—Phoenix, Sandy Fennerty, P. O. Box 9295, Phoenix, AZ 85068

First Independent Star Trekkers is "very interested in corresponding with other fans and organizations." They'll gladly answer questions on **Trek.** Write: F.I.S.T., c/o Mark Pugh, 2148 Madera Drive, Sierra Vista, AZ 85635

Tucson Star Trek Fan Association, 9701 East Colette Street, Tucson, AZ 85710

Arkansas

First Federation, Richard Robinson, P. O. Box 172, Dardanelle, AR 72834

California

STAR—Chatsworth, Robert Griffis, 9624 Oakdale, Chatsworth, CA 91311

STAR Klique, P. O. Box 433, Daly City, CA 94014

Vulcan Space Central, Ron Chang, 146 Arcacia Street, Daly City, CA 94014

Star Trek Freaks United, Melanie Mayfield, 805 M Street, Eureka, CA 95501

STAR-Fresno, Jon Golding, 3001 East Willis, Fresno, CA 93706

Stellax Universe, Patricia Stoddard, 2404 East Nutwood Avenue D-12, Fullerton, CA 92631

Starbase 1, Mark Chittenden, P. O. Box 1402, Glendora, CA 91740

Star Trek Association of Irvine is based on the Irvine campus, but its more than fifty members are nonstudents as well as University of California students. This community club is socially oriented. They meet to talk about **Trek** and related subjects. Activities: small con planning, car rally, volleyball and fizzbin tourneys. Write: STAI, Campus Organizational Services, 106 Gateway Commons, University of California, Irvine, CA 92717. Mark Bixby, Commander.

Star Fleet Club La Jolla, Paul Jacobs, 2710 Inverness Court, La Jolla, CA 92037

Terran League, S–F club of the Recreation Center at the Defense Language Institute, Presidio of Monterey. Members: civilians from the communities around the military base, men and women in the Army, Navy, Air Force, Marines, Coast Guard and civilian government personnel. Meets 2nd and 4th Tuesday, every month, 7:30 P.M. Has lively discussions, memorabilia displays, posters, info, con news. Box for S–F book exchange. Slide shows, film clips, con pix, films. Plays old radio S–F shows. Parties every few months with **ST** slides, trivia quizzes, taped greetings from cast members and taped Q. & A. sessions from cons. Sponsors **ST** parties at hospitals, youth centers, community centers, military posts, on request. No dues, no officers.

A star amongst the stars,
Uhura shines the
brightest, as illustrated by
Gee Moaven for Furaha.

Uhura and Scotty are
shocked by an alien
intruder's presence.
© Paramount Pictures
Corporation.

While under attack in another time zone, Captain Kirk calls for aid. © Paramount Pictures Corporation.

Captain Kirk tries in vain to communicate with the *Enterprise.* © Paramount Pictures Corporation.

Anyone, any age, is welcome. Talented artists Nancy Cris (who made the specimen "beasties" in McCoy's lab) and Dorris Quinn (winner of an award in the North American Sci-Fi Art Show) are members. Visitors to the area are welcome to drop by. Write: Program Director, Presidio Recreation Center, Presidio of Monterey, CA 93940, or call (408) 242-8516. Or write: Dorris Quinn, Program Director, Box 628, Pacific Grove, CA 93950.

Star Trek California, c/o Mike Herrera, 1186 Helen Drive, Milbrae, CA 94030

Star Base Eleven, Headquarters for the Nov-Sam Fan Club, is so called because it's based in Novato, CA but includes the Territory of American Samoa. President Terri Clark lived in American Samoa four years and says **Trek** was a favorite with natives and Americans. Membership: 7 in Samoa, 13 in Novato. No dues, just participation. NL, **The Enterprise Capers**, monthly. Officers: In addition to Terri, Sandra Mazciritis, Vice President Samoa, Leslie Whitt, Vice President Novato, Brad Carlson, Secretary, Steven P. Clark, Treasurer. Write: Terri Clark, 433 Estado Way, Novato, CA 94947, (415) 892-2220

Star Trek Association of Richmond, Karen Wetzler, 971 34 Street, Richmond, CA 94805

Federation Intelligence Agency, John Almada, 212 Dawnridge Road, Roseville, CA 95678

STAR—Sacramento Valley, P. O. Box 22584, Sacramento, CA 95822

The People of Vulcan, Terri Clawson, 5329 Dante Street, San Diego, CA 92117

Terra-Vulcan mainly explores Vulcan culture. Projects include a Vulcan puzzle book, language book, Vulcan calendar, poetry book, etc. NL bimonthly runs a forum on Vulcan culture to which members contribute. Also yearbook of Vulcan literature and art. Membership, 100, wide-

Ever calm, Uhura makes a terrific housemother for the *Enterprise*. Photo: UPI.

Next page:
The lovely Nichelle Nichols looks every bit the star at the 1976 ST Con held in Toronto. Photo courtesy of Stephen Halpert of Star Base One, Bloomfield Hills, Michigan.

spread in USA, Canada, West Germany, Japan. Write: President: Debra McWilliams, 2042 4th Avenue #5, San Diego, CA 92101

High Steppin' Trekkies, Outpost National, Adrienne Foster, P. O. Box 6783, San Jose, CA 95150

High Steppin' Trekkies, Outpost One, formed February 1976, is an outpost of HST National. Members, 22. Monthly meetings open to non-members as well. Their NL gives information about cons and all **Trek** activities in the Bay area. Write: HST, Daniel Biringer, 176 North 17th Street, San Jose, CA 95112

Star—San Jose, Mrs. Jerry Van Pelt, 1488 Phantom Avenue, San Jose, CA 95125

Star Base San Jose, Robert Dickerson, 250 Beegum Way, San Jose, CA 95123

Friends of Klingon, 14974 Osceola Street, Sylmar, CA 91342

Colorado

Far Out, J. Marshall, 275 South 38th, Boulder, CO 80303

Star Trek Fan Club, Danny Madsen, 930 Evanston Street, Aurora, CO 80011

Mile High Starship, launched June 1976. General interest club, meets second Tuesday of the month. Officers: Captain Dan Wagner, First Officer Flo Dubowitz, Yeoman /Paymaster Steven Waltz. Sounds like a highly "energized" group. Write: MHS, c /o Flo Dubowitz, 1250 South Monaco Parkway #79, Denver, CO 80224

Star Base Denver has about 20 active members who meet the first Friday of every month at St. Thomas Episcopal, 2201 Dexter, 7:30 P.M. Open to anyone. Activities: Built **Enterprise** bridge. Slide shows and demos; etc. Oldest continuous fan club for **ST** in Denver. Officers: President Daniel C. Bacon, Vice President Valerie Brickel, Secretary Mary Ann Sibley, Treasurer Judy Pimberton. Write: c /o Mary Ann Sibley, 115 South Emerson, Denver, CO 80209

Western State of Colorado Star Trek Club, James Jones, Mountain View Chalet, Apt. 20 117 North Taylor, Gunnison, CO 81230

Star Base Denver, Gail Barton, 31 Rangeview Drive, Lakeview, CO 80215

Connecticut

Galileo's 7 Club, formed in 1976 at the Kosciuszko Junior High School, 170 Elm Street, Enfield, CT 06082. Science teacher Andrew DePino, Jr., says the club's formation was the idea of one of his science students, Dan Deslaurier. Members, 22. Meets Thursdays after classes in the Captain's Quarters (Commodore DePino's classroom). Officers are changed every two weeks by a unique "election" formula: each member selects a **Trek** character's name out of a hat, then becomes that character for the next two weeks and takes on corresponding responsibilities—Kirk runs the meetings, for example. Zines written by members. "I have sponsored several after-school activities previously," DePino reports, "but *never* have I experienced the enthusiasm of these junior Trekkies! They really are into **ST**!" Sounds like a winning combo—eager, interested students with a responsive, encouraging teacher. Future NASA recruits?

Federation of Star Fleet, K. J. Chase, Route 341, Kent, CT 06757

Harcourt Fenton Mudd Android Society of America, a real fun club, founded February 1975. Serious, too. No regular meetings because members range all over the USA and into Canada. Locals did hold a Christmas party at which Saurian brandy (blue birch beer) was served. Rusty Judd and Clare Haney (pen names: Norman and Norma, after the android leader in "I, Mudd") are founders and officers. Club has about 20 members. Dues, $3.50,

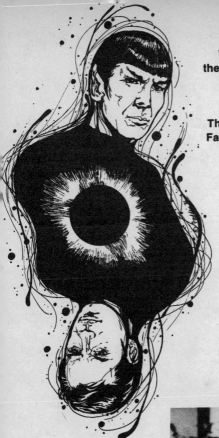

Bottom:
Without a doubt, this is the strangest chess board known to man. Photo: UPI.

The very talented Connie Faddis illustrates the universal bond between Spock and Kirk.

Nona uses her healing powers to save Kirk's life in "A Private Little War." Artist: Joni Wagner for Furaha.

Captain Kirk finds himself inundated with Tribbles in this famous episode "The Trouble with Tribbles." © Paramount Pictures Corporation.

don't go far so HFMASA sells 45-rpm records (**ST** themes), recorded by the Warp Nine group, to cover expenses. Send SAS envelope for info booklet. Rusty and Clare have been interviewed and written up in the *New Milford Times* and have been on two radio talk shows to play **ST** trivia and to discuss Trekdom. Address: HFMASA, P. O. Box 1073, New Milford, CT 06776

Delaware

Star Trek Club of Delaware County Community College, Media, DE 19063. Restricted to students of the school only.

Star Trek Association of Fans, 106 Radcliffe Drive, Neward, DE 19711

Florida

Transporter Enterprises, Douglas Krumbhaar, 514 Briarwood Court, Altamonte, FL 32701

Caloosa Star Trek Fan Club, Steven Ledbetter, 2910 Southeast 17th Avenue, Cape Coral, FL 33904

Star Trek Federation of Fans—Ft. Pierce, Mary Dymun, P. O. Box 3386 Ft. Pierce, FL 33450

Utrek, formed at University of Florida, March 1974. A student organization, chartered by the University of Florida Student Government. Therefore only UF students may join, though meetings are usually open to the public. No mail order memberships permitted. Members, 20 to 40 in number, are very changeable because the students graduate, transfer out, etc. Meetings discuss Vulcan history, the **Technical Manual**, fan fiction, show episodes, news of books, cons, etc. Address: 300 J. W. Reitz Union, University of Florida Campus, Gainesville, FL 32611

James Doohan is shown with Barbara Clipper and Adele Acosta at a recent Con. Photo courtesy of Miami chapter of STUFF, Opa Locka, Florida.

Right:

James Doohan looks pensive in this image of him reproduced by Creative Computing.

Star Trek Associated Florida Fans, 105 Martin Street, Indian Harbor Beach, FL 32935

The Association for Renewal of Star Trek, Box 1179, Hollywood, FL 33020

Star Trek Sector—Jacksonville, Danny Quitter, P. O. Box 5741, Jacksonville, FL 32205

Orlando Star Trek Club, c/o Enterprise One, 400 North Highway 1792, Longwood, FL 32750

STUFF, Broward Chapter #3, 5709 Northwest 23 Street, Margate, FL 33063

Florida Institute of Technology Society for Science Fiction and Fantasy (FITSSFF), a campus-based club, has avid interest in **ST** and S–F. Formed in 1972, it has 35 members who seem to move mountains. They've shown over 100 S–F films at least once to SRO audiences of over 1,000 at times. They've done two radio plays for the school's WFIT-FM station. Some zine staffers have press accreditation to cover events like NASA Skylab and

Apollo-Soyuz missions. Held their first one-day minicon (FITCON) in 1976, a huge success. Hope to cosponsor a stage production of Orwell's *1984* with FIT College Players and also **ST**'s "Requiem for Methuselah." The University will soon have a 3-credit liberal arts course on S–F theory and writing, thanks to cooperation of the Society and the school's Humanities Department. Officers: President Tony Boatright, Vice President Richard Engelbach, Secretary Isabella Macdonald, Treasurer Vienna Mackey, Zine Editor Mark Wardlow. Welcomes contact with other clubs or individuals. Write: FITSSFF, Campus Box 5597, F.I.T., Melbourne, FL 32901

Star Trek United Federation of Fans (STUFF)—Naples Chapter covers southern Florida for STUFF. Members, 25, and they really have fun! They love costume parties and put on a great show. Once a month, they go to Miami STUFF's minicons. Meet monthly for good times and to see a film. Officers: President Anne Malcolm, Vice President Randy Koger, Secretary-Treasurer Miriam Martinez, Board Member Rebecca Burke, Sergeant-at-arms Karen

Stewart. Officers are young adults. Write: STUFF, P. O. Box 7072, Naples, FL 33940

The Penetrators, Route 7, P. O. Box 256, Ocala, FL 32670 or 940 Southeast 28 Street, Ocala, FL 32670

Star Trek United Federation of Fans (STUFF)—Miami Chapter stresses that they're a non-profit club and mother club to 5 other chapters in Florida, New York and Texas, supplying them with membership cards and their NL, **Captain's Log**; otherwise, chapters operate independently. Meets 4th Friday of the month at the Museum of Science, 3280 North Miami Avenue. Door prizes, films, drawings and info of coming events and cons are regular meeting fare. Club, founded February 1974, has some interesting history, including **ST** romance and marriage. The daughter of Club President Barbara A. Clipper, herself a member, first met her husband at a con, and their wedding had an **ST** theme. The couple's daughter was made a member when she was one day old! Other officers: Vice Presidents Vince Mennella, Joseph Motes; Recording Secretary Bill Wrigley, Correspondence Secretary Adele

The Starfleet Graduate School Club artfully created its own insignia.

Acosta, Treasurer Lee Costello. Dues, below age 15, $3; age 16 and over, $5. Covers membership card, card holder, button, bimonthly **Captain's Log**. Write: STUFF, 3010 Northwest 153 Territory, Opa Locka, FL 33054. (305) 688-2991

United Fans of Penellas, begun July 1975, originally a chapter of STUFF. Membership, 200, growing and open to all ages. $5 annual dues. NL **USS Enterprise** is a monthly. Write: UFP, President Richard Clabaugh, P. O. Box 10354, St. Petersburg, FL 33733

People Allied for the Return of Star Trek, the Enterprise and Its Original Crew (PARSEC)—the name tells its purpose. A free-form group, no dues, no officers, no formal meetings—just mail contact and a meeting of creative, innovative minds. They're the mother organization of the Keroq Foundation. The Foundation raises money for cystic fibrosis, Nimoy's special charity. They also send funds to the American Cancer Society in memory of Gene L. Coon. Want contributions of short stories, poetry and art relating to Trekdom. Write: PARSEC, c/o Gail Saville, 925A Miccosukee Road, Tallahassee, FL 32303

Georgia

STAR—Georgia, Allan Crowe, 869 King Road, Stone Mountain, GA 30083

Valdosta Interstellar Star Trek Appreciation Society (VISTAS) is mostly interested in **ST** and *Space 1999*, especially their technology. Working toward a south Georgia con. Interested fans make contact. Members, about 20. Dues, $2, includes free subscription to NL **Trekkin' On**, (Non-members; NL is 15 ¢ a copy and $1.60 subscription, by hand; 25¢ a copy and $3 subscription by mail). Officers: President Tim Farley; Vice President Chas L. Martin; Secretary, Derek Pickup. Write: Tim Farley, 3001 Wendover Road, Valdosta, GA 31601

Idaho

Star Fleet Base 1, Teresa Sproul, 2401 Hill Road, Boise, ID 83702

Star Fleet Base 2, Susan Sackinger, 1006 East Wyeth, Pocatello, ID 83201

Star Trek Again, the oldest **ST** club in operation, originated August 1972, completed its 5-year mission August 1977. Activities: local TV ads, letter campaigns, NL **Star Trek this Month**, two annual zines, sales of stationery, rubber stamps, etc. Members, 200 nationwide. Club Director Lawrence Fury, Assistant Director Bob McCoy. Write: STA 615 Forest Avenue, Sandpoint, ID 83864

Illinois

Star Trek Lives, Rusty Grant, R.R. 1, Covered Bridge Road, Belleville, IL 62221

The Planet Orekton, Eleanor Walter, 2231 West Melrose Street, Chicago, IL 60618

Above:
Spock confers with Scotty on the illogical variance in the course of the *Enterprise.* © **Paramount Pictures Corporation.**

An excellent portrait of Mr. Spock, courtesy of Stardate: Unknown.

"Looks like the crew is ready for its big closeup, Mr. DeMille." And so begins another episode of ST. Photo: UPI.

Queen to Queen's Three is a private club with limited membership. Formed, August 1975. Concept: They're the crew of the new **Enterprise** with an eternal mission to bring peace wherever they go, and to go as far as they can. Meets monthly, dues $7.50 yearly, covers free NL **The Queen's Herald**, membership packet, unlimited access to their **ST** information center. Held minicon May 1976, Chicago. Motto: Peace to all planets. Officers: Captain Christina Smoron, Executive Officer Commander Don Adamaitis, Intelligence Officer Commander Susan Hebda; Lieutenant-Commanders: Michael Jencevice, Director of Finance; George Breo, Director of Communications; T.J. Smoron, Director of Secret Intelligence; Linda Hanson, Director of Publications. Junior Officers: Lieutenants: Christopher Schell, Personnel; Chris Coker, Communications; Barry Waterman, Communications; Sue Smith, Auxiliary Services. Write: Captain C. Smoron, Star Base 10, 1723 North Menard, Chicago, IL 60636

Starfleet Command, Dean Calin, 4427 North Artesian, Chicago, IL 60625

Starfleet Planetary Information Center, Eric Bradshaw, 11581 South Sangamon, Chicago, IL 60643

United Federation of Planets, founded April 27, 1976, in response to fans in the area, NL **The Federation Chronicle**'s first issue appeared on that date, too. That's organization! Members: 20 locally, 15 out of state. Main interest: The organizational and technical aspects of **ST** and other worthy S–F shows and books. Officers: Acting President Galen Beck, Vice President David Hawkins, Write: UFP, 398 Valley Drive, East Alton, IL 62024. (618) 259-0857

Kirk Fans Central, Mary Lelik, 2714B Center Street, Granite City, IL 62040

Chambana Sector, Guy Jackson, 4242 8th Avenue, Moline, IL 61265

Trekkies Unit, P. O. Box 511, Normal, IL 61761

Star Trek Association for Revival—Northbrook is the largest S.T.A.R. group in Illinois with well over 140 members. Founded December 1973 by Stuart Weiss. Dues, $3 a year. Meets 6 times annually. Group gets great newspaper publicity for Trekdom. An adult and student group. Write: STAR—Northbrook, 2906 Canterbury Drive, Northbrook, IL 60062

Trekster's Union, Karen Pouliot, 302 Pierce Street, Pontiac, IL 61764

That Which Survives, Scott Berfield, 671 Park Avenue East, Princeton, IL 61356

The Plant Orekton, Brad Brassfield, 3181 Andover Drive, Rockford, IL 61111

Star Trek Association of Fans—Illinois, Brad Brassfield, 3181 Andover Drive, Rockford, IL 61111

Making of Star Trek (MOST), 517 South 7th Street, St. Charles, IL 60174

Star Base 3, Randy Kaempen, 46 West 56th Street, Westmont, IL 60559

Indiana

STRAK, Lee Staton, 513 Mockingbird Drive, Jeffersonville, IN 47130

Star Base 6—Indy, Marlynn Skirvin, 7626 East 53rd Street, Lawrence, IN 46226

Star Trek Club of South Bend, founded May 1975, about 40 members. A lot of action here. Meets monthly to discuss activities, Trekdom, S–F and sci-fact. NL, **The Communicator**, available at $2 a year or 50 ¢ a copy. Planning a **Star Trek** and S–F zine. Will accept articles and art work. Send for info. Business Club Committee is responsible for **Trek** and S–F memorabilia and original models. Catalog available, 25¢. Officers: Phil Patnaude President-Captain, Stefan Sobol Vice President-First Officer, Sue Wells Communications Officer–NL Editor, Brian Jordan Treasurer-Navigation Officer, Betsy Brazy Engineering Officer-Business. Write the club: P. O. Box 422, South Bend, IN 46624

Iowa

STAR of Northwest Iowa, 28 East Park Street, Spencer, IA 51301

Iowa Star Trek Admiration Society, founded October 1975 by Linda Thieman, active member Welcommittee. 60 members, 10 out of state. Dues, $2 and 6 first class stamps, SAS envelope. Zine: **ISTAS Review**. 6 NLs and minizines a year. Officers: President and Editor of **Review** Linda Thieman, Contributing Editor Mark McDermott. Write: ISTAS, 610 Kelvin Road, Emerald Park, Storm Lake, IA 50588 (712) 732-6163

Kansas

Order to Unite Together for the Promotion and Organization of Star Trek (OUTPOST) has grown from its beginning 6 members at the end of 1975 to more than 75. They have many clubs in the USA and want more, more, more! Hold 2 cons a year, one for members, one for everyone. Age range is 9 to 35. Issues a semi-annual zine and monthly NL. Now here's their novel idea: to get all **Trek** fans throughout the world into one organization. Steven M. Hiser, International President. For info on the club or on how to start an OUTPOST member club, write them at 1615 North Belmont, Wichita, KS 67208

OUTPOST—Wichita, Dee Usio, 8540 Brookhollow, Wichita, KS 67208

OUTPOST—W.S.U., Debra Stroud, 2415 Wilma, Wichita, KS 67211

Kentucky

Social Workers for Star Trek, 3811 Blackburn Avenue, Ashland, KY 41101

Mercer County Star Trek Fan Club, 552 Beaumont Avenue, Harrodsburg, KY 40330

Louisiana

Star Base—Baton Rouge's membership of 200 has been growing steadily since their beginning in October 1975. Meetings, the third Saturday of the month. Range of age, 3 or 4 years to men and women in their 40s. At meetings, a favorite is a **Trek** episode, borrowed from local TV 33. Next are **ST** slides from various episodes; members bring them in. Have enjoyed speeches by Sandra Marshak and Myrna Culbreath, nationally known authors who live in the area. Write: SB-BR, c/o Mike Mengis, 1720 North Vega Drive, Baton Rouge, LA 70815

STAR Base—Baton Rouge, James Madden, P. O. Box 18610-A University Station, Baton Rouge, LA 70803. Local club.

Cosmica International: US, Michael Swan, 461 Beverly Gardens Drive, Metarie, LA 70001

Star Trek Club of Monroe, Thomas Barrett, 39 Lake Drive, Monroe, LA 71201

Star Trek Louisiana, c/o Gary Henigan, 411 Milam, Shreveport, LA 71101

Dr. McCoy as our surgeon in residence rarely loses a case. De-Forest Kelley's likeness reproduced by Creative Computing.

Next page:

Always busy when not on camera, Leonard Nimoy enjoys photography. Photo courtesy of *LNAF Yearbook,* for which this photo was the cover.

Science Fiction Society of Northeast Louisiana's 40 members meet twice monthly, Friday evenings. Usually, meetings include business, speaker, films, discussion. Plans amateur films, dramatic radio productions, possible regional con. Annual costume ball. Officers: President Brian Worthington, Vice President Marilyn Douglas, Secretary Nicki Gaines, Treasurer Mary Jo Worthington, Board: Jim Hendrixon, John Lowe, Tim Douglas. Write the club at: 1412 North McGuire, Monroe, LA 71203

Union of Ambassadors Star Trek Fan Club, Liz Ellen Snyder, 3616 Peachtree Street, Slidell, LA 70458

Vulcanis, Juanita Breeze, 430 College Street, Shreveport, LA 71104

Maine

Federation of Fans, a general interest club, formed in 1971, has 20 out-of-town members. NL **The Transporter**

is bimonthly. Plans are perking for a zine (needs material), a library and a museum of fan works. Write: President Richard W. Beebe II, 129 Main Street, Fryeburg, ME 04037. (207) 935-2398

Science Fiction Club of the Cosmos, Charles Jacques, 199 Payne Road, Scarborough, ME 04074

Maryland

Crew of the USS Excalibur, A.W. Glass, 2402 St. Paul Street, Baltimore, MD 21218. A local club.

University of Maryland Association of Star Trek (UM-AST), Maryland Student Union, College Park, Maryland 20742. Summer address: 1619 Ridout Road, Annapolis, MD 21401

Metro Area Star Trek Club (MAST), Polly Neulenberg, 8114 Fallow Drive, Gaithersburg, MD 20760

Keep on Trekkin', Warren Lievallen, 3125 Homework Parkway, Kensington, MD 20795

Mt. Airy Association for the Appreciation of Star Trek, Bill Miller, 504 Park Avenue, Route 5, Mt. Airy, MD 21771

Massachusetts

Star Trek Lives, Barbara Iwanski, 328 Van Meter South, University of Massachusetts, Amherst, MA 01002

Star Trek Andover Federation, Richard Leppert, 10 Olympia Way, Andover, MA 01810

Star Trek Correspondence Club, USA Representative Sandi Necchi, 73 Campbell Street, Fall River, MA 02723

Main Mission Alpha, Mary Hartery, 26 Asticou Road, Jamaica Plains, MA 02130

Boston Star Trek Association (BASTA), Gail Abend, 27 Michael Road, Randolph, MA 02368

South Hadley High School Star Trek Club, begun 1974. Hosts yearly minicon for students and guests. 40 members, meets 5 times yearly. Officers: President Ashley Roundtree, Vice President Dave Smith, Secretary-Treasurer Allan Farnham, Advisor William Gleason. Write: SHHS Star Trek club, c/o W.D. Gleason, South Hadley High School, 135 Newton Street, South Hadley, MA 01075. (413) 533-3943

Star Trek Club, c/o Mrs. Smith, Turners Falls High School, Turnpike Road, Turners Falls, MA 01376

McCoy's Scribes, Daphne Hamilton, 79 West Street, Worcester, MA 01609

Michigan

The Society of Earthborn Vulcans and Other Aliens, Phillip French, 210 East Chicago Street, Allen, MI 49227

Star Base One publishes a zine. Veteran clubber Stephen Halpert heads the group. Write him: 5501 Lakeview Drive, Bloomfield Hills, MI 48013

Beyond the Face of the Earth, 6808 James Street, Brown City, MI 48416

STAR—Charlotte, Don Howe, Route 6, Charlotte, MI 48813

ST—SF Club, Dearborn High School, Thomas General, 220 South Melborn, Dearborn, MI 48124

Friends of Star Trek, 19054 Toepfer East, Detroit, MI 48021

STAR—Detroit, Don Hall, 15830 Warwick, Detroit, MI 48224

STAR—Detroit, Wayne State University, W3F Box 102 UCB, Detroit, MI 48202

Star Flight Associates, Gary Stahl, 8253 Brace, Detroit, MI 48228

Michigan State University Star Trek Club, Lori Chapek, 559 Cornell Avenue, East Lansing, MI 48823

STAR—Lansing, John C. Evans, 3101 Glenbrook Drive, Lansing, MI 48910

Star Trek Fan Club of Grand Rapids, Dan Packard, 2121 Robinson Road Southeast, Grand Rapids, MI 49506

Star Trek Michigan, c/o Terry Griffith, 2122 Coolridge Road, Holt, MI 48842.

STAR—Northville, Elaine Hinman, Connie Miller, 760 Carpenter, Northville, MI 48167

STAR—Royal Oak, Star Base Antares, Chris Snyder, 3704 Kent, Royal Oak, MI 48013

Trekkies Unite, Diane Drutowski, 2412 Galpin, Royal Oak, MI 48073

Minnesota

Where No Fan Has Gone Before, Joe Ames, 8404 Shady View Lane, Osseo, MN 55369

The Penetrators, P. O. Box 642, Thief River Falls, MN 56701

Missouri

Trekkies United, 1824 Sergeant, Joplin, MO 64801

Mid-America Star Trek (MAST), P. O. Box 40, Station E, St. Joseph, MO 64505

FIRST-Missouri, Brad Hicks, 1371 Broadlawns Lane, St. Louis, MO 63138

Midwest International SF Info Team (MISFIT), Brad Hicks, 1371 Broadlawns Lane, St. Louis, MO 63138

Montana

Star Trek Intermountain—Butte, Jack Kusler, Jr., 1127 West Mercury Street, Butte, MT 59701

Nebraska

Starfleet Trinary Info Center (STIC), Patrick Jaderborg, PSC #2, Box 6409, Affutt Air Force Base, NE 68113

QUEI—Starmarian Network (QSN), P. O. Box 81571, Lincoln, NE 68501

Starbase Andromeda, STAR—Nebraska, P. O. Box 80064, Lincoln, NE 68501

Star Trekfan Club Leminicus, Agris Taurins, P. O. Box 80481, Lincoln, NE 68502

The UN—L ST Association, Room 200, Box 8, Nebraska Union, 14 and R Streets, University of Nebraska, Lincoln, NE 68508. Student and faculty members only.

Nevada

Idiots In Correspondence (IDIC) are trivia fans, that's for sure. They call themselves a simple "down home" club with no elaborate cosmic plans. As the name says, they're not a local but a correspondence club, ideal for isolated people. Voluntary "ranking" for members, based on trivia knowledge. Those who wish may take quizzes, moving from easy to harder questions, and will be ranked ensign, lieutenant, lieutenant-commander, commander, captain, commodore, admiral and a top level to be decided. Interesting and fun, too. Vice President is Jane Kaplan. Write: IDIC c/o President Constance Colman, P. O. Box 2016, Hawthorne, NV 89415.

Star Trek Intermountain—Las Vegas, Catherine Keegan, 1025 Yucca Street, Las Vegas, NV 89104

Star Trek Intermountain—Reno, Chris Kirby, 445 Linden Street, Reno, NV 89502

New Hampshire

Standard Orbit, Stephen Serieka, West Parish Road, Concord, NH 03301

New Jersey

New Jersey's Friends of Star Trek, has 10 members attending meetings held at least semi-monthly, and 17 corresponding members. They discuss various aspects of the **Trek** phenomenon and any news they may have about the series' stars. They attend lectures, cons, performances dealing with Trekdom and its stars. A forthcoming zine is still untitled. The group is open to all ages; present range is from 15 to 30 years. Officers: President Toni Cardinal, Vice President Marty Barquinero, Secretary Alicia Kagen, Treasurer Andy Pilote. Sounds like a live-wire group. Write NJ FOST, c/o Tony Cardinal, 13 Edgewater Beach Apartments, Beverly, NJ 08010

Nexus Club, c/o Marty Barquinero, EE2 Irongate Apartments, Beverly, NJ 08010

Cinnaminson Star Trek Fan Association, Tom Chidrestek, 702 Wood Lane, Cinnaminson, NJ 08077

United Mutations, formerly the Tribble Lovin' Hobbits is a correspondence club which answers questions concerning **Star Trek** and science fiction in general. For further information SAS envelope to United Mutations, c/o Sean Rockoff, 218 South Main Street, Hightstown, NJ 08520

Beyond the Stars is a Vulcan-oriented correspondence club interested mainly in communicating with people of like mind. Membership, 148 and far-flung, reaching to Australia, South Africa, Europe, Canada. Began in 1973 as a chapter of Leonard Nimoy Association of Fans. Do several NLs and a yearly zine. Members are encouraged to contribute. Officers: President Carolyn Venino, Co-President Stephanie Purvis, Vice Presidents Debbie Braun, Gizela Kent. Write the club at: 74 Palisade Avenue, Jersey City, NJ 07306

Star—New Jersey, Cathy Doyle, 3 Reed Road, Landing, NJ 07850

The World of Fantasy and Science Fiction operates from Livingston High as an in-school organization but accepts outside members. Since its origin in March 1975, the club has been busy with films, guest speakers, school window display called "2076, the Tricentennial." Officers:

President Barry Wolfe, Vice President Richard Pecht, Secretary Stephanie Rawson, Treasurer Dave Keisman, Coordinator David Lieberman. Write: WFASF, Stephanie Rawson, Secretary; 14 Knollwood Drive, Livingston, NJ 07039

Monmouth Science Fiction Society, Karen Constable, 4 Fayette Lane, Matawan, NJ 07747

Andorian Solution, Eric Weber, 162 East Street Andrews Drive, Moorestown, NJ 08057

Star Trek Outpost #1, Michael Strickle, P. O. Box 259, Newfoundland, NJ 07435

Memory Alpha Star Trek Club, Riverside Branch, c/o Roberta Rogow, Paterson Public Library, 254 Madison Avenue, Paterson, NJ 07514

Memory Beta Star Trek Club, c/o Paterson Free Public Library, 250 Broadway, Paterson, NJ 07501. Attn. Roberta Rogow

Vulcan Irregulars, Vivian Bregman, Store #200, West Belt Mall, Wayne, NJ 07470

West Orange Mountain High School Star Trek Club, J. Germansky, West Orange Mountain High School, 51 Conforti Avenue, West Orange, NJ 07052

New York

Star Trek Association of Fans, New York, Mark Croft, Rural Delivery #1, East Shore Circle, Ithaca, NY 14850

Terrans for Leonard Nimoy, started August 1974. Main focus is on Nimoy's activities. Members: 70, including 11 outside the USA. Dues, $3 a year. Publishes a yearbook and 3 zines a year with stories, articles, photos, cartoons, puzzles by members. Co-Presidents: Kyllikki Hodgden and Sue Bonnichsen (1661 Damen Street, Moscow, ID

quizzes and slide shows after meetings. Participates in local **Trek** events. Aided local public library in a **Star Trek** and Fandom display. Holds picnics, parties. Write: Commander Christine A. McWilliams, STAR Base Akron, 1160 Delia Avenue, Akron, OH 44320

Star Trek Club of America (STCA), Jonathan Bastock, 59 West Lowell Avenue, Akron, OH 44310

Bay Village Star Trek Association, 28505 Lincoln Drive, Bay Village, OH 44140

STAR—Bellaire, Vulcan Space Central, 3035 Washington Street, Bellaire, OH 43906

High Steppin' Trekkies, Outpost Two is mainly concerned with seriously exploring the philosophy and meaning of Trekdom through their publications and at meetings. Their NL **Cosmic Borders** examines one **Trek** episode in depth, also gives club news and general **Trek** news. NL is free to members; non-members may write for info on prices or trades. Activities: Club hopes to hold a con in Cincinnati and to have at least a half-hour TV program discussing Trekdom and its meaning to our society. Expect to have publications in the future. Membership, 25 and going up! Meetings monthly. Write: James T. Crawford, Vice President; OUTPOST Two, 4688 Marburg #3 Cincinnati, OH 45209

It Lives, Tony Roberto, 18028 Weston Road, Cleveland, OH 44121

The Star Trekkle, 4929 Fairway Court, Columbus, OH 43214

Shuttle Craft Columbus, Don Heil, 300 South Harris Avenue, Columbus, OH 43204

Star Base Dayton, 1595 North Fairfield, Dayton, OH 45432

Trekkers United Fan Club, formed in 1974. Just a bunch

of Trekkers, they say, who like **ST** a lot. That sounds cool. Publication. Write to: Bill Stratton, Jr., TUFC, 1557 Princeton Drive, Dayton, OH 45406

United Star Trek Society, 958 Harding Way East, Galion, OH 44833

Federation Crazy Corps, begun near the end of 1975, has relaxed set-up, no officers, a club for the fun of it. Meets every month at Toledo Pollution Control Building. Come sit in on the fun, discuss **ST** and S–F in literature and film, etc. NL **Federation Gazette**. About 20 members. Write: FCC, P. O. Box 97, Genoa, OH 43430. (419) 693-9158

Star Trek Federation Fans, Maple Heights Chapter have a going concern, a meeting place, 9 members and are anxious for more. Call Rick Bennet, President, for details at (216) 473-4976. Other officers: Vice President Frank Lucas, Executive Secretary Donald Spera. Write: STFF, Maple Heights Chapter, 19209 Beverly Avenue, Maple Heights, OH 44137

Officers of the Potemkin NCC 1711, James Powell, 6650 Stratford Road, Painesville, OH 44077

STAR—Dayton, Marla Garland, 7350 South Meadow Drive, Tipp City, OH 45371

United Federation of Star Trek Fans accepts any and all members who share similar interests in **ST**. No dues. Meetings are casual get-togethers. Members, about 10. Write: President Pam Jones, 4906 Elbon Road, Waynesville, OH 45068

Oklahoma

Claremore Association of Star Trek Fans Fan Club has 12 members who share a strong interest in Trekdom and S–F. NL, **News Around the Federation**. Officers: Captain

United Nations International Star Trek Association (UNISTAR) with about 250 members, is one of the largest NYC-based clubs. Officers: Fleet Admiral, retired Geoffrey Mandel; Admiral Imran Ahmed, Admiral Matisse Enzer. Activities: **Trek** revival (leaflet distribution, etc.), meetings at cons, pen-pal service, information /news center and exchange, **ST** and SF play productions ("The Trouble with Tribbles"). Founded January 1974. Publications: **UNISTAR**—monthly NL. **The Star Fleet Handbook**, bimonthly. Permanent HQ: United Nations International School, 24-50 East River Drive, New York, NY 10010. Mailing address: UNISTAR, c /o Geoffrey Mandel, 201 West 16th Street, Apartment 20A, NY, NY 10011

Vendikar, started February 1976. Meets Sundays. Much enthusiasm here. Officers: President Rosann Nicodemo, Secretary /Artist Gerard Stark; Officer Board: Terry Ornis, Karen MacCloud, Marja Stungurys, Barbara Adams. Write: Rosann Nicodemo, 73-23 53rd Avenue, Maspeth, NY 11378

Star Trek New York, M. Quinn, 104-27 88th Avenue, Richmond Hill, NY 11418

Memory Alpha II's a thriving group of 40, strong on discussions and publishing. NL **Time Portal**, bimonthly, 35¢ per issue. Meetings on irregular basis. Officers: Mike Warner, Jim Ward. Write the club at: P. O. Box 115, Ray Brook, NY 12977. (518) 891-1922

Star Trek Prospers meets the first Saturday of the month. Has about 100 members world-wide (England, Germany, etc.). They cover everything in fandom they can—including what the actors did before their **Trek** days, on stage, in movies, TV, etc. Monthly newszine carries poems, drawings, short stories, trivia—facts and fun. For info, send SAS envelope to: Joanne Bennett, STP, 425 Riverleigh Avenue, Riverhead, NY 11901

Association for the Propagation of Trekkism (APT), Lori Bartlett, 291 Ridgedale Circle, Rochester, NY 14616

Trek Fans Penpal Service is 40 members strong and getting stronger all the time. Founded in January 1976, it's open to **Trek**, S–F and fantasy fans. 30¢ and an SAS envelope puts you in the inner circle. Write the club c/o President Shelby Salzberg, 35 Arbor Road, Roslyn Heights, NY 11577

Scarsdale High School Star Trek Club, Jed Hilly, 272 Blvd., Scarsdale, NY 10583. Open to the school members only.

The Federation, David Solo, 4 Johns Road, Setauket, NY 11733

STAR—Syracuse, Carl Norman, 113 Alanson, Syracuse, NY 13207

Affiliated Star Trek Revival Organization, 137 Hoosick Street, Troy, NY 21280

Trek Pals, Alex Bonziglia, 1065 Fulton Street, Woodmere, NY 11598

North Carolina

Star Base 17, P. O. Box 392, Faith, NC 28041

Ohio

Star Trek Association for Revival—Base Akron (STAR) is mainly concerned with the return of **ST** and the promotion of good S–F. Formed December 1974 by advertising in the Akron University paper. Bimonthly NL **STAR Base Akron's Log** gets great reviews. Club meets monthly, Saturdays, 2 P.M. Dues, $5 a year, subscription $4 (subject to change). This lively group holds audio trivia

83843). Write Kyllikki Hodgden for membership and sub-
scriptions at: P. O. Box 2, 110 Halcyon Hill, Ithaca, NY
14850

Starbase Suffolk, Debbie Myers, 18 Tallow Lane, Lake
Grove, NY 11755

Enterprise Irregulars, Susan Palmstrom, P. O. Box 663,
Lake Ronkonkoma, NY 11779

Leonard Nimoy Association of Fans (Chapter LN—New
York), Judith Breen, 424 Parker Avenue, Levittown, NY
11756

Starbase Omicron, Holly Pratt, 124 Sargent Lane, Liver-
pool, NY 13088

New York City clubs

Loyal Order of Trekkers, 2710 Webb Avenue, Bronx, NY
10468

Star Fleet Graduate School, The Star Trek club of the
Bronx High School of Science. Begun in February 1976,

After conferring with Dr. McCoy, Captain Kirk issues orders to destroy the alien force. © Paramount Pictures Corporation.

the club has about 70 members. Original idea was to use students' scientific specialization to produce supplemental technical orders to the Franz Joseph **Technical Manual**, but fans at Science High were interested in more than the technology of Trekdom, so they became a general interest club. Officers: Commander Andres Castineiras, Commandant: Staff Members: Sheldon Ranz, Joseph DiBenedetto, John Gallagher, Peter Squires. Members meet once or twice a month. They welcome correspondence members. Send SAS envelope to: SFGS, c/o Andres Castineiras, 222 Newman Avenue, Bronx, NY 10473

United Federation of Star Trek, Timothy Brevoort, 5534 D Street, Apt. 3C, Brooklyn, NY 11208

Star Trek Pen Friends, Elena Offsey, 1721 Dahill Road, Brooklyn, NY 11223

Star Trek Revival Fan Club, welcomes inquiries along with an SAS envelope. Write: Louis Matteo Jr., 1900 New York Avenue, Brooklyn, NY 11210 (212) 252-1269

Steve Warren, First Officer Jeff Jones. Address the club: Route 1, Box 479, Claremore, OK 74017. (918) 341-5302

United Federation of Planets, founded July 8, 1975 by Tony Behrens and Eddie Cunningham. NL **Captain's Log** monthly. Basically a correspondence club and info center. Membership, $2.50, covers 12 issues of the NL and half the price of their zine. Working on pen-pal operation. Address: UFP, 2429 Knox Drive, Del City, OK 73115

Starbase Enid, Robert Abiera, 305 University Boulevard, Enid, OK 73701

Moore Organization of Star Trek (MOST), local club with the accent on meetings and interaction. Meets 3rd Saturday of the month at Moore Public Library. Members must be in 6th grade or over and must attend meetings. Dues, 50¢ a month. NL **Starpower** is a monthly, 75¢ a copy, free to members. Editor, David Thornburg. Held garage sales to raise money to launch the club, and they've been in business since September 1976. Officers: President Dawn Atkins, Treasurer Doug Madden, Secretary

Steve Pursley. Write: MOST, c/o Dawn Atkins, 825 North West 7th, Moore, OK 73160

STAR—Oklahoma City, Daryl Maxwell, 2205 Markwell Place, Oklahoma City, OK 73127

STAR—Tulsa, 6709 East 29th Street, Tulsa, OK 74129

Star Trek Again, Mrs. Ron J. Frantz, Post Office Box 95171, Oklahoma City, OK 73109

Oregon

Federation Council, 252 Lamb Road, Elmira, OR 97347

Pennsylvania

Star Trek Correspondence Club, Brenda Stamper, 412 Shetland Road, Darby, PA 19023

The Second Age, formed May 1975. P. O. Box 265, Dresher, PA 19025

Me Club has special activities for local members. They invite other **Trek** and S—F fans at times to meet the members, with a view to recruiting. Most activities are social parties. Sounds like fun. They play **Trek**-oriented games, like a **Trek** version of the *$10,000 Pyramid*. Hold an annual summer swim—wiener roast party, hosted by various club members. Mainly interested in getting members to know one another by personal contact or through pen-pals. 29 members at present. Membership $2 a year. Covers 6 issues of the zine, film clips, photo stamps, membership card. Each new member gets a personal gift—like a photo of his /her favorite star or Vulcan crystals. Write: Tinz Olszak, The Me Club, Box 19, Fenelton, PA 16034 **Trek**, Rural Delivery 4, P. O. Box 346, Hummelstown, PA 17036

The Kahn-ut-tu People, Bonnie Guyan, 502 Dorothy Avenue, Johnstown, PA 15906

The Organian Entity, Woodrow Wilson High School, 3001 Green Lane, Levittown, PA 19057

Star Trek Fan Club of New Castle, Pennsylvania began with 3 people in late 1975. An ad in the local paper advertised their meeting. "The next day, we got a call from one of the reporters asking if they could include us in a 3-page feature on **Star Trek**. Since then, it's been warp 10 all the way!" They publish the **Pennsylvania Star Times**. Goal is to get all Pennsylvania clubs together in an effort to bring **Star Trek** back on the air. Meets once a month. Small (9 members) but "we have big ideas," they say. Officers: President Chris Dwyer, Treasurer Rob Brest, Secretary Danny Fore. Address: Star Trek Fan Club, 2911 Rosedale Avenue, New Castle, PA 16105

Leonard's Pennsy and Otherwise Freaks is a loosely structured correspondence club. Very nominal dues. About 100 members of all ages. Club is an offshoot of the Leonard Nimoy Association of Fans. Write: c /o Becca

On location for "The Paradise Syndrome"—the view from behind the cameras (left) and how it looks on your TV screen. © Paramount Pictures Corporation.

Oroukin, 13693 Ormsby Drive, North Huntingdon, PA
15642

Where No Fan Has Gone Before is an information service with a small **Trek** revival campaign. Founded September 1975 with the help of Chris Buelow, 6761 Cotton-
wood Lane, Maple Grove, MN 55369; Chris Anderson,
6754 Evergreen Lane, Maple Grove, MN 55369; David
Hainlin, 7108 Willow Road, North Maple Grove, MN 55369
and Rick Dolinsky, RR 3, Box 313, Tamaqua, PA 18252.
If you would like information about **ST**, write to one of the
above or to: President Joseph Ames, WNFHGB, Rural Delivery 2, New Ringgold, PA 17960

Central Star Command, Scott Benson, Penn Towers
Apt. 1603, Philadelphia, PA 19103

Lincoln Star Fleet, 2607 Welsh Road, Heritage Park
Apartments 1-101, Philadelphia, PA 19152

STAR—Pittsburgh, Vicky Mandel, 1614 Denniston Avenue, Pittsburgh, PA 15217

Spring—Ford Star Trek Club, Joseph Kessler, Advisor,
Spring—Ford High School, Royersford, PA 19468

University of Scranton Star Trek Fan Club, Mary Alice
McCormack, 736 River Street, Scranton, PA 18505

United Federation of Star Trek Fans, Scott Stevens,
HUB Desk, University Park, PA 16802

Rhode Island

The Star Trek Club of Roger Williams College officially
became a branch of Star Fleet Embassy, Providence, RI
(see listing below). Officers: Captain Fred Dimauro, Commander Michael Gerrity, Lieutenant-Commander Denis La
Freniere, Pleeb Gary Taitz. Write the club at: Room 2320,
3 North, Roger Williams College, Bristol, RI 02809

Star Fleet Embassy began in 1975 as Computer Circuitry, a branch of **Star Trek: Revival**. Members, 30. Now SFE has a branch of its own, the Star Trek Club of Roger Williams College. Bimonthly NL, **Star Fleet Ambassador**. Interested in setting up tape, letter and membership exchanges with overseas *Trek* clubs. Hope to set up Rhode Island's first con. Officers: Commander Nancy Spargo, Science Officer Patrick Lynch, Chief Engineer Dino Larson, Helmsman Sharon Makokian, Navigator Cathy Voll. Write: SFE, P. O. Box 2906 North Station, Providence, RI 02908

South Carolina

United Federation of South Carolina Trekkies, Vicki Plaxico, 106 Hampton Avenue, Gaffney, SC 29340

Trek, 330 West Market Street, Graham, SC 27253

Star Trek: Again—South Carolina, Rebecca Hoffman, 205 Pine Street, Greer, SC 29651 (See listing below)

Greenville Association of Star Trek Fans, also known as **Star Trek: Again—South Carolina**. Meets the third Friday of every month in the public library conference room, Greenville, from 7 to 9 P.M. No dues; instead, they pass the hat. They're mostly a rap club, about 40 members, from 15 to college age and a few near 30. Informal club, no officers. Have had displays and sales set-ups in local malls to publicize the club and have shown blooper reels. Send SAS envelope to: Rebecca Hoffman, 205 Pine Street, Greer, SC 29651

Menagerie, JoAnn Atwood, RR 1, Box 285-L, Laurie Bay, SC 29902

STAF—South Carolina, Pat Berry, 512 Guilford Road, Rock Hill, SC 29730

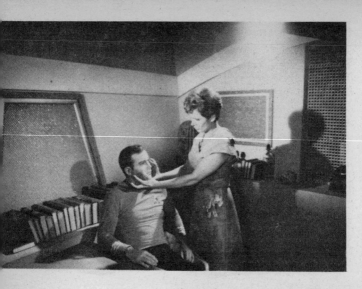

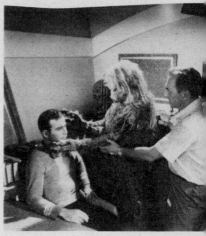

The two faces of the monster in "The Man Trap." In these shots, Jeanny Bal as Nancy Crater begins the scene with William Shatner, then the apelike beast is positioned for the transformation effect. © Paramount Pictures Corporation.

South Dakota

Star Trek Nuts is a club with science fiction, fantasy, and related subjects as aims, with primary emphasis on **Star Trek**. Discussion and activities are encouraged.

Star Trek Nuts is divided into five types of members. Local members, automatically on the Lower Council, meet at irregular intervals, and are responsible for all legislative decisions. A select group of local members, called the High Council, is responsible for calling meetings and executive decisions. There are no dues for local members, and with membership, both Lower and High Council receive a membership card, a listing in the pen-pal list, and a discount price (subtraction of postage costs) on the NL, **Star Trek Nuts and Bolts**.

The last three types of membership are for out-of-town members. Full active membership requires yearly dues of $3.25, and includes a membership card, filmclips, listing in the pen-pal list, and six free issues of **Star Trek Nuts and Bolts** the zine. "String" active members requires bimonthly dues of 60¢ or four 15¢ stamps, and brings the member all the benefits of full active membership. Semi-active membership requires no dues, and the member receives a membership card and a listing in the pen-pal list.

A complete listing of all new members is published in each issue of **Star Trek Nuts and Bolts**. At the end of each year, all members for that year are published in a separate listing. Lists are available for 75¢ each, postage paid.

Membership is open to all. To join, send a check for the proper amount (payable to George Perkins or Mark Behrend) along with the following information for the pen-pal list: name, address, phone number (include area code), age, birthday, favorite: Star Trek character, guest star, episode, piece of equipment and set. Star Trek Nuts, George Perkins, 1102 Third Street, Brookings, SD 57006

Tennessee

Allies for Star Trek, P. O. Box 388, Forest Hills, TN 38031

Nashville Science Fiction Club (Nashville Starbase), David Winfrey, High Route 1, Greenbrier, TN 37073

Eastern Science Fiction Association, Eric Jamborski, P. O. Box 358, Harriman, TN 37748

Star Trek Fan Club Branch A, 2005 Hermitage Drive, Kingsport, TN 37664

Star Trek Commission for Revival (STCR), Mark Widener, 2005 Hermitage Drive, Kingsport, TN 37664

STAR—Knoxville, Susan Baker, P. O. Box 22, 821 Volunteer Boulevard, Knoxville, TN 37916

TEXAS

Galaxy's Edge, Darlene Johnson, 2490 Loop 35, #1514, Alvin, TX 77511

Man's Sojourn Through the Future, 2545 Mimosa, Abilene, TX 79603

Vulstar, Trek and S—F club, open to all, from Orion to beyond Antares. Purpose: to promote understanding and appreciation of Trekdom and its philosophy, and to give an opportunity to express the philosophy artistically. Officers: Admiral Teresa Patterson, Commander I Jas Robinson, Commander II Cindy Grinstead, Communications Officer Julie West, Captain of Treasury Robt. Richter. Write: Vulstar, 4015 Pleasant Ridge, Arlington, TX 76016

Watchers and Fans of Star Trek Society, Outpost #2, c/o Tim Wallace, 817 McCurry, Bedford, TX 76021. See WAFSTS listing for Headquarters group in Dallas, below, for details of the organization.

East Texas State University Star Trek Club, John Lamb, 2812 McCarley, Commerce, TX 75428

The Confederation of Fandom, originally the Planet Orekton, was set up in February 1974. Members, about 25, meet every other week. Members range—from age 14 to a grandmother of 6. Youngest member, Elliott Sanford, has won several trivia cash-prize contests in Texas. Members are nurses, teachers, writers, engineers, film makers, computer operators, students from all over Dallas. Club helps local cons as aides, doing trivia contest and art shows for them. Their annual New Year's Eve dinner is a highlight. They dig into S–F, movies, comics, fantasy, etc. but dig **ST** most. A proud and happy club. Write CFF, c/o C.A. Thompson, 604 Vernet Street, Richardson, TX 75080. (214) 235-1465

Romulan Tape Corresponders, Robert Stucker, 1109 Glencliffe Drive, Dallas TX 75217

The Watchers and Fans of Star Trek Society (WAFSTS), founded 7411.06. 100 members strong and growing! A rundown of their activities explains. First, members need only send SAS envelope with every letter, and they get an answer. Every member is doing something exciting—working on the pen-pal service, on the zine, or building working communications and tricorders for personal use. At cons, they run a "comlink" system, a network of CB radios. Helps locate family, friends and **ST** personalities at cons. Has outposts in Chicago, West Dallas, Bedford (Texas) and Guam. Others forming in Holland and Hawaii, possibly. Officers: President Richard Secrist, Vice President C. Robert Stevens, Executive Staff: Lynn Secrist, Bill Madison, Tom Murphy. World Executive: Debborah Goldthwaite (Los Angeles), Chris Smoron (Chicago), Bill Bailey, John Davis (West Dallas), Tim Wallace (Bedford, Texas), Victor Leach (Guam). Write to: WAFSTS, c/o Richard Secrist, 7139 Winterwood Lane, Dallas, TX 75248

Metro Star Trek Club, Richard Stanley, 5612 Wales, Fort Worth, TX 76133

Nimoyan/Spock's Scribes, Donna Humberd, 3462 West Gambrill, Fort Worth, TX 76133

Star Trek Keepers, Mike Hoover and Kathy Carr, 12419 Old Oaks, Houston, TX 77024

Texas Star Trek Questors, 6939 Capitol Avenue, Trailer #9, Houston, TX 77011

United Federation of Star Trek Followers, Jack Jones, 4103 Wuthering Heights, Houston, TX 77045

Worshippers of Walter (WOW), Brenda Horn, 601 Sesame Lane, Laredo, TX 78041

Starfleet has over 400 members in 31 states, Canada and West Germany. Dues, $3 a year; renewals $2.50. Formed October 1974 as the USS Enterprise, mainly a local club. In May 1975, it became Starfleet, a national organization. In the pattern of **ST**'s Starfleet, members are assigned to starships and ground installations with service ranks, official positions and serial numbers. Membership packet tells about the club and its activities; membership card is patterned after **ST**'s identity card. Bimonthly NL **Starfleet Communications**. Projects: Starfleet Census, a survey of all **Trek** fans. Send SAS envelope for form Starfleet Academy, their most ambitious project, will include a training manual of all facets of starship operations, starfleet technology, operation and Federation culture. Officers: John Bradbury, Chief of Staff, Starfleet Command; Admiral Peggy Goins, Chief of Operations; Admiral Warren Scherffius, Chief of Technology; Commander Stephanie Purvis, Starfleet Census. Write: Starfleet Central, 104 Hemlock Road, Lufkin, TX 75901

Starfleet Command, John Bradbury, 104 Hemlock Road, Lufkin, TX 75901

Leonard Nimoy
and Louise Stange
at the 1976 New
York ST Con.
Photo courtesy of
Louise Stange,
Leonard Nimoy
Association of
Fans.

Bottom:
Catspaw, with il-
lustrations by
Tony Boatright,
the fan club at the
Florida Institute of
Technology.

Live Long And Prosper

USS Enterprise, 2202 Peachtree Street, Lufkin, TX 75901

STAR—Houston, 18335 Carriage Lane, Nassau Bay, TX 77058

Save the Star Trek Cast, P. O. Box 3432, Pasadena, TX 77502

What Star Trek Is Made Of (WSTIMO), Route 1, Box 220, Rockwall, TX 75087

San Antonio Star Trek Club, Michael Smith, 1611 Alice Hill, San Antonio, TX 78232

San Antonio Star Trek Fan Club, Doug Bauer, 104 Tomahawk Trail, San Antonio, TX 78323

The Star League, Cheryl Solis, 210 West Ware, San Antonio, TX 78211

STAR—Texas, Bill Patterson, 9615 Bryce, Waco, TX 76710

Utah

Star Trek—Intermountain/Logan, Dorothy Nelson, 657 East 300 South, Hyrum, UT 84319

Regulus Prime, P. O. Box 18643, Kearns, UT 84118

United Federation of Star Trek—Related Clubs, Carol Andrus, 4411 West 5010 South, Kearns, UT 84118

STAR—Utah Valley, Diane Howarth, 1095 South 545 East, Orem, UT 84147

USS Excalibur, 330 East 800 North, Provo, UT 84601

Star Trek Intermountain, P. O. Box 11066, Salt Lake City, UT 84147

Vermont

Vermont Star Trek Organization, Lynn Holland, 108 Lost Nation Road, Essex Junction, VT 05452

Virginia

Freeworld Associates, a **Trek** and S–F club founded in 1974 by Curtis Phillips. NL published randomly. Bi-yearly zine. No dues. The founder says, "Through the efforts of the members, we have instituted a science fiction class in a local high school." For more info, send SAS envelope to: Curtis Phillips, Route 1 Box 219, Abingdon, VA 24210

Enterprise: Frontiers, 3527 Paul Street, Alexandria, VA 22311

Trekkie Truckers Star Trek Club, P. O. Box 521, Stuarts Draft, VA 24477

Washington

Olympia Affiliated Fans, Rob Kimmel, 6418 37th Lane South East, Lacey, WA 98502

Star Trek, Kathleen Rock, 716 Fisherman's Loop, Burlington, WA 98233

Puget Sound Star Trekkers, Incorporated (7510.17). With 1,000 members in the Northwest, its yearly meeting is so big it's called a con, and is it ever a good one! Headquarters (Star Base 7) is in Seattle, with 16 outposts in Washington, Oregon and British Columbia which meet weekly or monthly. PSST is a heart-and-mind organization involved in community and **ST** projects. **Trek** activities: 1. Building—a captain's chair, Doomsday machine, Horta, other models. 2. Printing—3 zines and distinctive blue stationery. 3. Publicity—petitions and the con. The Communi-

Furaha, the official Nichelle Nichols fan club, captures its magazine readers both visually and rhetorically with handsome covers such as the above. Artist: Constance R. Faddis. Cover courtesy of Furaha.

Next page:
At an Intergalactic reception, Spock discusses his skepticism to the amusement of Kirk and McCoy.
© Paramount Pictures Corporation.

ty Support Project (Alkoran) is mind-blowing! Includes: regular blood bank donations, aluminum recycling, sponsoring a foster child in India, periodic collection of food for local Food Bank (Neighbors in Need). A one-month Trekker-Treating campaign netted *one ton of food!* They practice 23rd-century morality in the 20th-century Northwest, USA. It works, and it's beautiful! Write: President Kit Canterbury, PSST, 6207 7th Avenue Northwest, Seattle, WA 98107

Wisconsin

Unlimited Star Trek Club, Cathy Shappe, 510 Leroy Road, Madison, WI 53704

Minocqua, Bob Ham, Jr., P. O. Box 593, Minocqua, WI 54548

Star Trek Fan Association (STFA), 861 South Park Street, Richland Center, WI 53581

Shazam, University of Whitewater, P. O. Box 119, University Center, Whitewater, WI 53190

Wyoming

Star Trekkers, Gregory Sherwood, P. O. Box 794, Glenrock, WY 82637

The Star Trek Mini Club, P. O. Box 418, Linden, WY 82520

Canada

Starfleet Trinary Information Center, Victoria, British Columbia branch. Officially known as CIRC #1 (Communications & Information Center), pronounced "Kirk." One of its many facets is the USS **Hektor**, NCC (listed in **The Starfleet Technical Manual**—TO:01:04:03) a 200-person complement, destroyer class vessel (Type VIIIB) Cochise class. The purpose of the **Hektor** and ships like her is to stimulate activity in **ST** and S–F. There are openings in the command section for helmsman, yeoman, navigator, ordinance specialists. Also need scientists, lab technicians, yeomen, doctors, nurses, medical technicians, engineering and transporter room specialists, communications officers. Submit the following information to join the **Hektor**: name, age, sex, personal past, experience with Star Fleet, desired position. CIRC #1 is made up of people living near each other but was started with letter-writing. Write: Richard Bronson, 443 Superior, Apt. 102, Victoria, British Columbia, V8V 4S7 Canada; Frank Alongi, 1927 Yuma, Mount Prospect, IL. USA 60056; Carolyn Ruth, 12900 Barto Drive, Granada Hills, CA, USA 91344; Carl Jan, 4211 Morgan Cres, Prince George, British Columbia, Canada

People of Star Trek, founded 1973. Activities: a minicon, (Models, filmclips, etc.), showing of pics, posters and life-size sets. Mainly a general **Trek** club "but being Canadian, we lean toward William Shatner and James Doohan." Understandable. Club officers: Tony Leblanc, Craig Carleton, Jeff Carleton. Address: P. O. S. T., 165 Jones Street, Moncton, New Brunswick, CA E1C 6K1. Phone: 506—382-7540. Collect calls cannot be accepted. Also understandable.

Star Trek Correspondence Club, Claudia Crawford, P. O. Box 1176, Sackville, New Brunswick, Canada

Loyalists of Star Trek (LOST) is the first all-Canadian club with membership open to Canadians only. Yearly dues, $2, includes club NL, membership card, certificate, **ST** film clips, a year's subscription to the zines. American and foreign subscriptions are accepted for the zines. Many new projects are in the works—bumper stickers, an annual, etc. Assistance and advice are appreciated. Send money order with membership application to: Ravi Prakash, Chairman, LOST, P. O. Box 977, Middleton, New South Canada B0S 1P0

STAR—Windsor, Patti Helmer, 173 Sandwich Street, Amherstburg, Ontario, Canada N9V 1Z9

Society for Earthbound Vulcans, founded to offer those

who consider themselves to be Vulcan a means to communicate with other Vulcans in this society. Aim is also to incorporate Vulcan lifestyle in music, art, language, philosophy, etc., as much as possible. Council of Elders: Head Elder, T'Pela, Elders: Sadoc, T'Lyn, T'Pon; Ambassador T'Leri, Council Secretary-Treasurer T'Py. To join, a person must be Vulcan or Terran with sincere wish to learn the Vulcan way, and must choose a Vulcan name, be over 14. No dues. Meets irregularly. NL **Mind-Meld**, monthly, 15¢ for members, 25¢ for others. Zine plus books and booklets on Vulcan language, arts, science, technology, philosophy, etc. For members only. To join this international society, write: Joy Fenton, Head Elder, 51 Fagan Drive, Georgetown, Ontario, Canada L7G 4P4

Star Trekkers Are Reviving (STAR)—Ontario helped energize Toronto **ST** '76 Con, the first Canadian con and a spectacular one. Club meets weekly, publishes zine. Write: Elizabeth Pierce, All Saints Circle, Oakville, Ontario, Canada

STAR—Ontario, Gary Cambridge, 81 Central Avenue #23, London, Ontario, Canada N6A 1M3

Star Trek Ontario, c/o Lynn Miller, 40 Hillsmount Road, London, Ontario, Canada N6K 1W2

Canadian Trekkle Association, founded Stardate 7601.03 by Susan Schmidt (unofficial president) and Laurel Russwurm, to share Trekdom and to publish a zine. Meets Tuesdays, centered in Elmira. Write: Susan Schmidt, CTA, P. O. Box 174, St. Jacobs, Ontario, Canada N0B 2ND

Amalgamated Canadian Trekkies (ACT), 1319 Rosemarie Avenue, Sudbury, Ontario, Canada P3A 4E4

S3 HQ, 1319 Rosemarie Avenue, Sudbury, Ontario, Canada P3A 4E4

Puerto Rico

Star Trek Team Club, Pedro Ramon, Calle 20 N-19, Magnolia Gardens, Bayomin, Puerto Rico 00619

When writing to any foreign club listed below, send international money orders instead of stamps, along with a self-addressed envelope.

France

Cosmica International, European Headquarters, Alexandria Gruber, #24, 36 Rue Henri Duhame, Village Olympique, 38100, Grenoble, France

Great Britain

Beyond Antares, Sheila Hull, 35 Merley Ways, Wimborne, Dorset, England BH21 1QN. Send 2 International money orders with letters.

Star Trek Action Group (STAG), Janet Quarton, 15 Letter Daill, Cairnbaan Lochilphead, Argyll, Scotland

Star Trek Enterprises Branch (STERB), oldest club in Britain, formed in 1972. Have issued 27 NLs to date. Co-directors: John Hind, Michael Rossiter. Write: STERB, 14 Bingham Road, Radcliffe-on-Trent, Nottingham, NG12 2FU, England

Starbase 13, begun 11/75. Bimonthly NL, **View Screen**; Quarterly NL, **Phaser Blasts**. Mascot, a Shelat called Enoch T. Jockstrap. Honorary Member, Gene Roddenberry. Zine Artists: Paul Dakeyne and Martyn Delaney. Pen Pal Secretary, Katrina Fletcher; Treasurer, Mrs. J. Longstaff; President, Brian Longstaff. Membership 50 plus. Write: Headquarters 13, Woodfarm Drive, Sheffield S6 5LW, South Yorkshire, England

Star Trek Correspondence Club (STCC), Jackie Dunham, 105 Sumerleighton Gardens, Norwich, England

Japan

Star Trek Club of Japan, c/o Yoshiko Hirahara, c/o Otorii-South Apartment, 111-21 Otorii-cho, Nishino Yamashina-ku, Kyoto 707 Japan

West Germany

United Federation of Star Trek Appreciators, Leonard May, c/o Brecht, 43 Essenbredeney, Seippelweg 11, West Germany

Star Trek Central Europe, c/o Ricky Eisen, Schubertstrausse 20, 8901 Westheim, West Germany

World-wide fan clubs for **ST** cast members are listed below alphabetically. Please remember SAS envelope when writing to any club.

James Doohan International Fan Club, Anna Hreha, 1519 North 204 Street, Seattle, WA 98177. An authorized and official organization. Pen-pal service, annual publication and NL, 5 times a year.

Mariette Hartley Fan Network—Mariette, who guest starred as Zarabeth in the **ST** third-season episode "All Our Yesterdays," cooperates and helps this club, her only official fan group. The club gives advance notice of her appearances, issues periodic journals **Hartlines** with photos, news, reviews of her recent work. Also gives personal information and has a section for members' comments and questions to Mariette. They sponsor fund-raising projects like raffles, proceeds going to Leader Dogs for the Blind, whose school is in Rochester, MI. Write: Rusty Hancock, MHFN, 1649 Longfellow Court, Rochester, MI 48063. Membership $3.50—includes intro kit (membership card, bio and credits and 8x10 photo of Mariette), 3 journals with all the news about Mariette. Foreign members, $5.

DeForest Kelley Association of Fans' packet for new members consists of: 8x10 photo of Kelley, membership card, photo button and NL six times a year. Write: DKAF c/o Karolyn Popovich, 1000 South Bryant, Denver, CO 80219

Walter Koenig Fan Club. Walter has given full approval to the club, provides it with current news of himself and co-operates as much as time allows. Dues, $4 annually USA, $5 Canada and overseas (use international money order, available at post office). Members receive: summer/fall and Christmas NL, spring yearbook—4x5 pic of Chekov, membership card, bio, stickers from Walter himself. Members may work at fan club table at **ST** cons and get a WKFC T-shirt to wear; they may also enter club contests. Chekov posters, $1.50; 8x10 b&w autographed photos, $1.25. Officers: President Jack L. Townsend, Vice President Patti Heylin, and Secretary Susan Houck, Route 7, Box 195, Lenior, NC 28645 (704) 754-6167

Mark Lenard International Fan Club goes back to May 1968, founded with Mark's cooperation, and continues to grow. $3 yearly membership. USA; $4 overseas. NL **The Despatch** appears 3 times annually, as news of Mark and circumstances permit. Volunteers for area captain post are welcome to help with the volume of mail. Members are invited to send articles about Lenard; identify the source. Fiction, verse, artwork, etc., featuring ML are fine. New members receive: card, certificate, 8x10 photo and introductory booklet. Write Gail Saville/Barbara Metzke, P. O. Box 1018, Tallahassee, FL 32302

Above:

Kirk confronts a glamorous opponent in this episode. Artist: Joni Wagner for Furaha.

Captain Kirk fell for this lovely lady (Barbara Anderson) not knowing that she had a deadly secret. Photo: UPI.

The ST Cons are an invaluable outlet for memorabilia collectors and merchandisers. Mr. Jeffry Gleich sells the controversial Decicentennial buttons. Photo: Maje Waldo.

Nichelle Nichols Fan Club's prime directive is to keep members updated on her activities and to open a channel of communication between her and her fans. Letters to her are forwarded. Club publishes bimonthly NL **Amani** (Swahili for peace); **Furaha** (joy) 3 times a year, and yearbook, **Uzuri** (beauty). Membership: $4 a year includes signed photo of Nichelle, card, welcome booklet, everything but **Furaha**. $8 members receive **Furaha** too, at half the subscription rate. Foreign membership, $5. A very active club with many original ideas and beautiful publications. See Nichelle's bio for info on club's fund-raising for charity. Club raises money by selling stationery and a 60-minute tape of Nichelle's out-of-print record album **Down to Earth**. For pen-pal info, send an additional SAS envelope. First Officer, Virginia Walker; Second Officer, Harry Friedenberg; Third Officer, Sharon Ferraro; Special Projects Officer, Fran Hitchcock. Write: NNFC, Virginia Walker, P. O. Drawer #350, Ayer, MA 01432

Leonard Nimoy Association of Fans welcomes and has members all over the world, 3500 of them! Nimoy's only official club dates from February 1967. He and his able

George Takei, Leonard Nimoy and James Doohan are welcome guests at all the Cons. This was at the 1973 New York Con. Photo: New Eye Studios.

aide Teresa Victor keep in close touch, with news of his upcoming appearances, TV and stage shows, films, books, etc. Club publishes NLs, bulletins and a yearbook to which multi-talented Nimoy himself contributes articles, photos, poetry, artwork. The Alan Nimoy Memorial Fund is the group's official charity, in memory of Leonard's nephew who died of cystic fibrosis at 17. Fans contribute to the fund instead of sending Leonard gifts and cards. It provides scholarships and a monthly sum to the Children's Hospital of Boston (Leonard's home town) for little extras for long-term patients. Profits from sale of club calendar and a book. Dues, $3 yearly, yield bulletins, NLs, yearbook, photo of Leonard, photo membership card, welcome booklet and the club's most recent publication. Overseas members must send international money order or bank money order. Write: LNAF, Louise Stange, President; 4612 Denver Court, Englewood, OH 45322

United Friends of William Shatner, authorized by Bill in 1975. He and wife Marcy are honorary president and vice president respectively. Club keeps members up on Bill's doings and appearances. Also alerts fans to cons, new

Trek products and books. Quarterly NL **All About Bill** is a justified point of pride with them. They issue **Green Alert** bulletins when important matters can't wait for the next NL. Activities on behalf of needy earthlings, especially children, are heartwarming. $1 of dues goes to Muscular Dystrophy, and other funds go to it, too. Also to Cerebral Palsy, Easter Seal Telethon. Two hundred mentally retarded children in a home in Montreal (Bill's home town) were picked for Christmas gifts. Membership, now 250, grows steadily. They meet at cons when they can. Funds are raised by selling stationery and patches. The group gives special thanks to Joan Winston, who helped them get started. Officers: President, Maxine Broadwater, a delightful dynamo; Vice President, Sharon Krause; Secretary, Barbara Calestini; Treasurer, Ann J. Lopiano; Photographer, Ann C. Teipen; Special Projects, Ruth Ann Wain. Richmond, VA President, Tina Deyerle; English President, Marjorie Moore; Japanese President, Yasuko Harada; Order Department, Adelaide Wind. Write: Mrs. Ron J. Frantz, Post Office Box 95171, Oklahoma City, Oklahoma 73109

Hosato, USA is the American branch of the British fan club founded for George Takei in 1974. Has George's cooperation and sanction. Hosato is George's middle name and means "village of the bountiful harvest." Since Hosato USA started in January 1976, it has indeed reaped a bountiful harvest—120 members and fans from all over the world. They hold business meetings monthly, but general membership is too widespread to meet; they communicate by mail and are represented at most major **ST** cons. A "Win Some Time with Mr. Sulu" raffle raises funds for the National Wildlife Federation, one of George's favorite charities. Club keeps up with his many activities and covers all phases of Trekdom. Their journal is **Ichi-Ban** (Japanese for "Number One") and their insignia is a dragon. Registered International Council of Fan Clubs. Dues, $4 a year

USA and Canada; $6 overseas. Includes: welcome packet, letter from George, membership card, NL **Ichi-Ban**, pen-pals, photos, yearbook and your questions personally answered by George. Outside USA, send international money orders. Officers: President, Kathy Bayne; Additional officers: Karen Hargrove, Cheryl McDaniel, Bobbi Stark, Ellen Mortimer and Polly Bayne. Write to: Kathy Bayne, 41-09 53rd Street, Woodside, NY 11377

Grace Lee Whitney Fan Club sends new members welcome letter, photo membership card, NL four times a year, 8x10 picture of Grace. Club is official and authorized. Richard Arnold, P. O. Box 7796, Van Nuys, CA 91409

Lovely Grace Lee Whitney in her role as Yeoman Janice Rand. © Paramount Pictures Corporation.

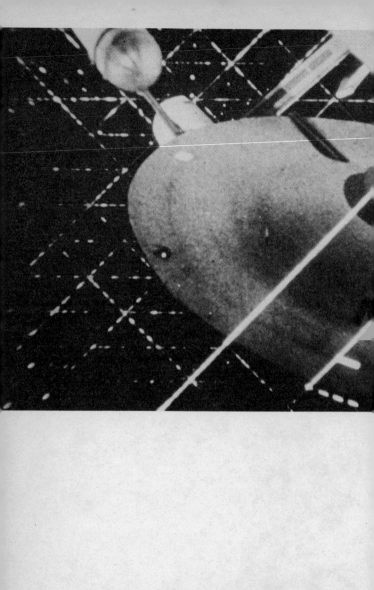

The Crew

William Shatner— Captain James T. Kirk, Commander, USS Enterprise

You watch talented, handsome, charismatic Bill Shatner in command on the bridge of the **Enterprise**, and you're sure he has all the style and looks of a born actor. But he wasn't one. In fact, it took him the entire first eight years of his life to come to the decision to act.

Young Bill was in summer camp then, and he had the lead role in an anti-Nazi play. As he tells it, "I was so truly affected, that I did a heart-stirring job. Had all the other kids and their parents crying their eyes out. That's when I first knew I wanted to be an actor."

Back from camp, Bill went to Children's Professional School in Canada, and for years afterwards he had parts in fairy-tale programs and in an adult series on Canadian radio. By the time he entered McGill University in his native Montreal, he was a well-known, very popular radio star.

At McGill, Bill wrote, produced, and acted for the campus theatrical group—and shone in all three jobs. He spent vacations in summer stock at the Mount Royal Playhouse. Then, in his senior year, he made his big announcement to his family. . . .

Though he had majored in business at college, and though he was the Shatner's only son (there were two daughters), Bill said he would not go into the family's very successful clothing manufacturing business; he'd go into the theater instead.

For weeks, Gerald Shatner tried to argue some sense into his son, to convince him he would not live long and prosper as an actor. But once his mind was made up, Bill was as determined as Captain Kirk. In the end, the father had to make a deal with his son. If, after five years, Bill didn't make it in acting, he'd go into the business.

Those next five years were both good and bad for Bill. He became one of Canada's most distinguished Shakespearean actors. Right after graduation, in 1952, he had joined the Canadian National Repertory Theatre in Ottawa, where he piled up many acting credits but little cash —thirty-one dollars a week, to be exact. His father again pleaded with him to give up the struggle and join him in the business. "But I refused to be discouraged," Bill says, and he went on to join the Stratford (Ontario) Shakespeare Festival. In a short time, audiences were giving this twenty-two-year-old newcomer standing ovations.

Sooner than he expected, Bill was Broadway-bound. The Festival took its fine production of *Tamburlaine* to New York City, cast and all. Though Big Apple theater goers were cool to the play, audiences and critics alike warmed up to Bill. Result: 20th Century—Fox offered him a seven-year contract, which he refused. "I wanted to be independent, to choose my own roles," he says, and he headed back to Toronto to do great plays rather than money-making, run-of-the-mill movies.

Back with the company, Bill met and married actress Gloria Rand in 1956. They had a working honeymoon in England, then went to New York. There Bill's exceptional talents were well-used in many first-class shows of the Golden Age of TV—*Omnibus, Philco Television Playhouse, Studio One, Playhouse 90, Alcoa Theater*, etc.

Above:
Captain Kirk alerts the crew of the presence of alien beings aboard the *Enterprise*. © Paramount Pictures Corporation.

Everyone's hero, Captain Kirk, has been skillfully reproduced by the Creative Computing firm of Morristown, New Jersey.

Bill's film debut followed, a fine portrayal in *The Brothers Karamazov* with Yul Brynner, Claire Bloom, and Lee J. Cobb. As a result of that and his outstanding TV work, he landed the male lead in Broadway's *The World of Suzie Wong,* a two-year smash hit. Critics called him a real find for his great acting and good looks. Two more plays, *A Shot in the Dark* and *L'Idiote,* kept him in New York awhile.

In the next few years, Bill piled up an enormous list of acting credits. There were movies—many westerns, *Judgment at Nuremberg* with Spencer Tracy, *The Intruder.* By this time, Bill was the father of three darling daughters —Leslie Carol, Lisabeth Mary, and Melanie Ann—and he knew he had to face the moment of truth as far as his career was concerned. Should he shelve his dream of being a great classical actor and stay in Hollywood where the financial security was? With much regret, he turned down juicy roles at Stratford to remain in Hollywood where movie and TV producers would be aware of him.

The year was 1965, and things were not going well for Bill. CBS was dropping the series *For the People,* in which he starred as district attorney. It was a good show, Bill said, but up against *Bonanza,* it couldn't get the ratings. For the first time, he began to lose parts. He was going through a disheartening time. Then, along came **Star Trek**. . . .

At that time, Bill was considering taking his father's advice belatedly, he told a *TV Guide* reporter (as quoted in the issue of June 22, 1968) and chucking acting to go into something else, if **Star Trek** didn't sell. "Maybe selling ties in Macy's," he said wryly. The series did sell, as everyone well knows. . . .

Apparently, though, **Trek**'s demanding schedule didn't do Bill's marriage much good. He and Gloria were separated after ten years of marriage and divorced after thirteen. Seven years later, on October 20, 1973, Bill married the beautiful Marcy Lafferty. You may have seen her with him in the TV margarine commercial. His official fan club officers who deal with Marcy love her, not only for the fine person she is, but because she's keeping him so happy.

Since **Trek** production ended, Bill has been very busy with speaking engagements at schools and cons. He's good at TV game shows like *The $25,000 Pyramid* because he's both intelligent and witty. He has hosted the *Challenge* celebrity sports series on TV and starred in the *Barbary Coast* Series. In the midst of all that, he founded his own production company, Lemli Productions, named in honor of his daughters, Leslie, Melanie, and Lisabeth, with whom he has always remained close. Of course, now there's the **Star Trek** movie to add to the list.

Bill has always been a big one for hobbies, busy or not, and he's very skillful at them—archery, waterskiing, snow skiing, motorcycling, scuba diving, raising Doberman pinschers, play writing, TV scripting, photography, collecting paintings, weight lifting, bareback riding, golf, and cross-country flying. Amazingly, he soloed after only eight hours of flying lessons. He also reads extensively.

To sum up William Shatner—our respected, admired, indomitable Captain Kirk—we quote his wife Marcy: "This man is fantastic!" she told the *National Enquirer.* "He's very strong, very male, very handsome and has great acting talent. I love him." What can we add but—you're so right, Marcy!

Facts of Life:

Real name: William Shatner
Birthplace: Montreal, Quebec, Canada
Birthdate: March 22, 1931 (Aries)
Weight: 160
Height: 5'11''
Hair: Light brown
Eyes: Hazel

Major acting credits

Stage: Canadian National Repertory Theatre, Stratford, Ontario Shakespeare Festival, Broadway—*The World of Suzie Wong, A Shot in the Dark, Tamburlaine.*
Movies: *The Brothers Karamazov, Judgment at Nuremberg, The Intruder,* many westerns.
TV: *Goodyear Theater, Studio One, Philco Television Playhouse, Naked City, Route 66, Omnibus, The Outer Limits, Family Classics Theatre (Scarlet Pimpernel), The U.S. Steel Hour, The Man from U.N.C.L.E., The Defenders, The Dick Powell Theater, 77 Sunset Strip, Alfred Hitchcock Presents, Alcoa Playhouse, The Nurses, Dr. Kildare, For the People, The Barbary Coast,* and others.

Preceding page: Captain Kirk in his Romulan disguise for "The Enterprise Incident." © Paramount Pictures Corporation.

Captain Kirk attempts to short-circuit chief android Norman while Harry Mudd looks on in a scene from "I, Mudd." © Paramount Pictures Corporation.

The Leonard Nimoy As-
sociation of Fans
courteously allowed us to
reprint this candid shot of
everyone's Mr. Spock,
which was included in its
1973 yearbook.

Leonard Nimoy—Mr. Spock, First Officer and Science Officer, USS Enterprise

Four days after Bill Shatner was born in Montreal, Leonard Nimoy gave a newborn lusty yell in Boston, Massachusetts, March 26, 1931. Leonard had his first taste of acting at eight (in *Hansel and Gretel*). At sixteen, he knew what he wanted—to be an actor. He studied drama at Boston University on a scholarship but dropped out at eighteen, impatient to get to Hollywood and "the real thing."

At the Pasadena Playhouse, Leonard studied for six months, then tried to break into acting while he "earned a living," more or less, selling vacuum cleaners, delivering newspapers, soda-jerking, cab-driving, working in a pet shop, ushering at theaters. The best thing that happened to him during that time was meeting actress Sandra Zober and marrying her.

The Nimoys left Los Angeles for Atlanta at Uncle Sam's "invitation." Leonard did a hitch in the army Special Services, putting on shows for the men. Daughter Julie was born in 1955; a year later, son Adam arrived. When Leonard was discharged, the family headed straight back to Los Angeles, where the TV and movie acting jobs were.

At first, there was much of the same waiting for a break and scrounging out a living in low-paying jobs of the kind Leonard had taken before. Then he began to teach acting, and meanwhile, a few good TV roles came along: *Dr. Kildare, The Virginian, Rawhide, The Outer Limits.* He also broke the movie barrier with *Seven Days in May* and *The Balcony.* It was all upward and onward then, but as Nimoy himself put it, he never had a steady job in seventeen years of show biz till **Star Trek**.

Gene Roddenberry, who produced the TV series *The Lieutenant,* had been deeply impressed with a guest role Nimoy had done for the show; with his remarkable casting ability, Gene knew Nimoy and Spock were made for one another. Immediately, the avalanche of fan mail directed at Spock-Nimoy proved it. Though the series has long been cancelled, the fan mail still pours in.

At the close of **ST**, Nimoy was immediately signed for the *Mission: Impossible* series; he stuck with it for two years, then broke out of his contract, finding the lack of challenge unbearable. He passed up a load of money, but it was worth it to him. As soon as he was free, he plunged seriously into photography and became a fine camera artist. Then it was back to his real love, the theater; playing Tevye in *Fiddler on the Roof* was one of Nimoy's greatest acting joys. He also made ten albums of poetry, prose, and music in the nine years after **Star Trek**.

The syndicated series *In Search Of. . .* had the good fortune to land Nimoy as host-narrator. It's a high-quality show that will probably be rerun on TV forever.

In the days since **Star Trek**, Nimoy has done a re-markable job of developing his hobbies into professions; first it was photography, then writing poetry and prose. See the book section for a list of his books, beautifully written and supplied with his exquisite photography.

Nimoy is a remarkable man—a teacher, director, artist-photographer, gifted writer, sensitive poet, a brilliant actor and fine human being who takes a courageous stand for

The many faces of Mr. Spock enhanced each episode. Illustration courtesy of the Leonard Nimoy Association of Fans, from its 1971 yearbook.

LNAF 71

Top:
No, you didn't miss this episode. This is a photo of Leonard Nimoy taken at the Federated Trading Post in New York while he was preparing to go on tour with a play in which he portrayed Sherlock Holmes. Photo: UPI.

his beliefs, which are uncannily close to **Trek** philosophy. Nimoy wasn't content to be against war in general; during the days of the Vietnam war, he was active in his opposition to it. He supports political candidates who reflect his philosophy of peace and equality. And with it all goes a delightful wit. It's almost too much to have in one human, even if he is half Vulcan.

Facts of Life:

Real name: Leonard Nimoy
Birthplace: Boston, Massachusetts
Birthdate: March 26, 1931 (Aries)
Height: 6 '
Weight: 165
Eyes: Brown
Hair: Brown

Major acting credits:

Stage: Toured with: *Fiddler on the Roof, Oliver, 6 Rms Rvr Vu, Full Circle* (Broadway), *Caligula, Man in the Glass Booth, The Fourposter, Camelot, The King and I, One Flew Over the Cuckoo's Nest, Equus* (Broadway), and others.
Movies: *The Brain Eaters, Queen for a Day, Catlow, The Balcony.*
TV: *Rawhide, The Virginian, Dr. Kildare, Outer Limits, Profiles in Courage, West Point, Bonanza, M. Squad, Sea Hunt, Wagon Train, Perry Mason, Gunsmoke, The Kraft Suspense Theater, The Man from U.N.C.L.E., The Lieutenant, Get Smart, Columbo, In Search Of.*

"Gentlemen, this is what I call a carburetor!" Photo: Wide World.

Impervious to the illogical, Mr. Spock looks out at us via the Creative Computing technique.

DeForest Kelley—Dr. Leonard "Bones" McCoy, Chief Medical Officer, USS Enterprise

The medical profession's loss was surely the entertainment world's gain when DeForest Kelley, who had once seriously considered a career as a doctor and was encouraged in it by his parents, decided to drop it for acting. Happily, he was able to combine both careers later in life in his three-year role as Dr. McCoy of the **Enterprise**, a man whose wit was as sharp as his scalpel.

De made his big career decision when he was seventeen, a year after he was graduated from high school in his native Atlanta, Georgia. He had gone to visit an uncle in Long Beach, California, De's first venture outside his home state. Instead of staying for only the scheduled two weeks, he stayed for an entire year, captivated by the life there. During that year, he made his big decision to become an actor.

It wasn't easy for him to go home and break the news to his parents. De's father, a Baptist minister, was not at all happy with the decision. But De's mother had learned to appreciate her son's theatrical talent long before, and she had actively encouraged him. In fact, she had helped him

find his place in the church choir where he had eventually become a soloist. His singing won him a spot on local radio station WSB and later an engagement at the Atlanta Paramount Theater, singing with Lew Forbes and his orchestra.

Back in California, De plunged into work. He joined the Long Beach Theater Group and put on a radio show with his friend Barney Girard. They appeared together on the local station, but the money did not flow in by any means. De had to work as an elevator operator on the side to keep going.

During World War II, Kelley made a training film while he was in the U.S. Navy. He did so well in the movie that he caught the eye of a Paramount Pictures talent scout. Later, upon his discharge from the navy, he was offered a screen test—and it led to a contract.

Luck held out, and so did De's talent. His first starring role was in a low-budget film, *Fear in the Night*. It turned out to be one of those wonderful box-office sleepers, a real hit that established him as a respected actor. He was well on his way up—it seemed.

After two and a half years with Paramount, in 1948, De struck out for New York City to get experience in stock theater, on the legitimate stage, and in TV (then in its childhood). Afterward, when he returned to Hollywood, he found he had to make a new start. That fickle town had just about forgotten him except for his old friend Barney Girard, who was writing TV scripts for the series *You Are There*. Barney quickly had De signed up for several of those shows. TV assignments came through steadily after that in *Gunsmoke, Schlitz Playhouse of Stars, Navy Log, Rawhide, Bonanza*, and others.

Kelley piled up movie credits, too—such as *Tension at Table Rock, Gunfight at the O.K. Corral, Raintree County*.

His lovely wife, Carolyn Dowling Kelley, had been with De since his early struggle to establish himself as an actor and through the years of success. They were married September 7, 1945. They met during a production of *The Innocent Young Man* given by the Long Beach Theater Group. Carolyn was an actress then, but she gave up her career.

After twenty years in TV, in films, and on stage portraying villains, "bad guys," and psychopaths, De landed the part of witty, sensible, and outspoken Dr. Leonard "Bones" McCoy, Senior Ship's Surgeon of the **Enterprise**, a first-class hero.

De is a big hit with the fans, not only because they love him in the part of "Bones," but because he's also a fine human being, full of warmth and humor. On the series's set, time after time, he cracked up the entire cast and crew with his jokes, and the stories got around to the fans. At cons, they were mesmerized by the obvious kindness and warmth of the man, his willingness to show his deep emotional responses, in a very unSpockian way, when he spoke to the crowds. They love him for it.

After **Trek** ended production, De took a long, well-deserved vacation. He has made some movies and done some TV—*Ironside, The Cowboys*—and he's been a smash hit in many appearances at dinner theaters, mainly in the Southwest. And of course there are the cons, where he meets his devoted, loyal, and still-growing number of fans.

Facts of Life:

Birthplace: Atlanta, Georgia
Birthday: January 20 (Capricorn)
Weight: 158
Height: 6 '
Hair: Brown
Eyes: Blue

Major acting credits:

Movies: *Tension at Table Rock, Gunfight at the O.K. Corral, Raintree County, The Law and Jake Wade, Warlock, Where Love Has Gone, Apache Uprising, Waco, Black Spurs, Town Tamers.*
TV: *Studio One, The Armstrong Circle Theater, The Web, Crime Syndicated, Danger, The Plainclothesman, Matinee Theater, Schlitz Playhouse of Stars, Dick Powell's Zane Grey Theater, Wanted—Dead or Alive, You Are There* (12 shows), *The Silent Service, Navy Log, O'Henry Playhouse, Gunsmoke, Arrest and Trial, 26 Men, Rawhide, Playhouse 90, Bonanza, The Chrysler Theater, The FBI, The Virginian.*

2/18/75.

#DD10

DeForest Kelley *

(I looked at a photo taken of him at the '74 N.Y.C. I.S.T.Con.)

©Eleni Vafías

Eleni Vaflas of the Puget Sound Star Trekkers contributed her interpretation of a photo taken of DeForest Kelley at the New York 1974 I.S.T. Con.

James Doohan— Chief Engineering Officer, Lieutenant Montgomery ("Scotty) Scott, USS Enterprise

If actors wore harsh marks for service, Jimmy Doohan would look like a zebra. Without counting his many **Star Trek** performances, he's made something like 400 TV appearances, acted in at least 125 plays, and done over 3500 radio shows! Plus films, both in Hollywood and for the Canadian National Film Board. In his "spare time," he taught for three years at an acting school in New York. You have to be good to be in demand like that!

In the profession, Jimmy is famous for his ability to handle dialects and foreign accents; as you can see—or hear—his Scottish brogue is just perfect.

Like William Shatner, Jimmy is Canadian-born—Vancouver, British Columbia—and he's very special to Canadian fans. USA Trekkers also warm to this hearty, good-humored man. Fans at the American **ST** con in Dallas, Halloween 1976, gave him and his wife Wende a warm welcome, especially when Jimmy exhibited their newborn son, Eric Montgomery Doohan, arrived stardate 7608.22. Jimmy has twin sons and two daughters by a previous marriage.

Many good things have happened to Doohan in the post—**Star Trek** days. He remarried, for one. He's grown a beard and moustache and looks terrific in them. He's still working hard at his craft, doing plays, TV commercials, some cons. He always was one of the most in demand actors in the field, and it looks like he always will be. When it comes to acting, this highly energized man knows only one way—warp 10!

Jim always enjoys the Cons and his devoted following, as shown in this photo taken at the New York ST Con in 1976 by Maje Waldo.

Facts of Life:

Birthplace: Vancouver, British Columbia
Birthday: March 3 (Pisces)
Weight: 165
Height: 5'10''
Hair: Dark Brown
Eyes: Hazel

Major acting credits:

It is impossible to single out even the important ones in this long and remarkable career. We'll just mention some of the more popular TV series, aside from **ST**, of course: *Ben Casey, Bonanza, Peyton Place, Gunsmoke*. Get the idea?

George Takel—Mr. Sulu, Helmsman and Weapons Officer, USS Enterprise

This capable, unflappable starship helmsman is in real life a third-generation American of mixed Oriental and Filipino background. When he was three, the United States was at war with Japan. Apparently our government decided that the Takei family was Japanese enough to be "relocated" from their Los Angeles home to a Santa Anita internment camp, then to another in the Arkansas swamps, and finally to one near northern California's Mount Shasta. George says he still remembers the barbed wire and high guard towers.

His parents told the children they were taking "a long vacation in the country." Years later, they told him, his brother, and his sister what "relocation" really meant. "It was a stunning revelation," George said.

In spite of this rough start, Takei had enough talent, intelligence, and grit to come out on top. He went to UCLA, studied architecture and city planning, then switched to theater arts. Even before he graduated in 1960, he landed a part in TV's prestigious *Playhouse 90*.

Nevertheless, George still had to go through the ordeal of a beginning actor—the training, job seeking, scrounging

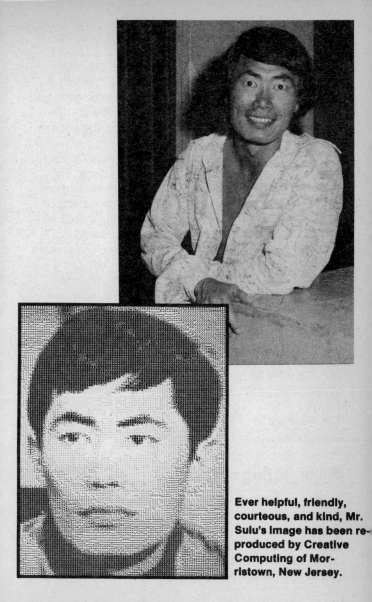

Ever helpful, friendly, courteous, and kind, Mr. Sulu's image has been reproduced by Creative Computing of Morristown, New Jersey.

for a living with only occasional acting jobs. Then TV found him. And so did the movies. It was fortunate for all that Gene Roddenberry also found him.

When the **Trek** series ended, Helmsman Sulu began steering a new course. His city planning background at UCLA helped Los Angeles's Mayor Bradley decide to appoint him a director of the South California Rapid Transit District. George also ran for City Council; he lost, but narrowly.

With all that activity, Takei still keeps a heavy TV schedule. He moderates a Saturday afternoon TV show, *Expression—East-West,* does guest appearances, and has some fine dramatic parts, as in the *Theater in America* play *The Year of the Dragon.* He also makes time for hobbies—fencing, painting, hiking, reading, camping, bicycling. In addition he's president of the Wilshire Chapter Japanese--American Citizen's League, and Vice-chairman of the Friends of Far Eastern Art of the Los Angeles County Museum (of which he's founding chairman).

Facts of Life:

Birthplace: Los Angeles, California
Birthday: April 20 (Aries)
Weight: 135
Height: 5'7½''
Hair: Black
Eyes: Brown

Major acting credits:

TV: *Playhouse 90, Perry Mason, Hawaiian Eye, The Islanders, Alcoa Premiere, Mr. Novak, I Spy, Checkmate, Khan, Six Million Dollar Man, O'Hara, U.S. Treasury, Theater in America (The Year of the Dragon),* plus many others.
Movies: *Ice Palace, A Majority of One, From Here to Eternity, The Green Berets.*

Nichelle Nichols— Lieutenant Uhura, Communications Officer, USS Enterprise

Nichelle unfortunately had few chances on **Star Trek** to show what a fine actress she is. But in the few instances when she had an opportunity to say something other than "Hailing frequencies open, Captain," she was splendid: for instance, in two brief scenes in "The Tholian Web" she did a superb job.

Not only is Ms. Nichols an accomplished actress, she has a singing voice of unusual range—fantastic, really— and she puts over a song with genuine artistry. In fact she was good enough to tour the USA, Canada, and Europe with Duke Ellington's and Lionel Hampton's bands.

Nichelle is also a first-class dancer. She was, in fact, the first black ballerina to be offered a contract at the Metropolitan Opera House. But she turned it down because at the time jazz, modern, and ethnic dance intrigued her more than ballet.

Gene Roddenberry gave Nichelle her first TV feature role, in *The Lieutenant,* and she proved so good he signed her up for **Star Trek**. It's not surprising that her fan mail, which still pours in, includes many marriage proposals. But Nichelle is still single.

Never fear when Uhura is near her control panel. The lovely Nichelle Nichols has been reproduced by the Creative Computing firm.

Facts of Life:

She was born in Robbins, Illinois, a town founded in the 1890s by black and integrated couples. Her paternal grandfather was a redheaded Welshman. When he was disinherited for marrying Nichelle's black grandmother, he changed his name from Gillespie to Nichols. Nichelle's father became magistrate of Robbins, and eventually mayor. In that same spirit of public service, Nichelle helped found the Kwanza (Swahili for spirit of giving) Foundation, an organization of black actresses serving Watts in Los Angeles. They started with giving turkeys and toys at holiday time but now serve year round, raising funds for hospital equipment. Kwanza is Nichelle's fan club's official charity.

Her hobbies are sculpting, designing and making her own clothes, tennis, the arts, and astronomy, and she's very good at them! She lives in Beverly Hills, was born December 28 (Capricorn), keeps two Siamese cats. She's the proud mother of actor-singer-musician-composer Kyle Johnson, who is handsome and talented and forging ahead in TV, theater, and film. Talent runs in the family.

Major acting credits:

Stage: Twice nominated for the Sarah Siddons Award as best actress of the year for *Kicks and Co.* and *The Blacks; Carmen Jones, Roar of the Greasepaint . . .* , *For My People, Blues for Mr. Charlie.*
TV: *The Lieutenant.*
Night clubs: Blue Angel, New York Playboy Club.

Walter Koenig— Ensign Paul Chekov, Navigator, USS Enterprise

Ever since production of **Star Trek** ended, Walter Koenig has gone boldly where he had never gone before. The very handsome, dashing Ensign Chekov—special favorite of so many female **Trek** fans—has been exploring and expanding his creative horizons, producing, directing, and writing a novel, movie and TV scripts ("The Infinite Vulcan" for the animated series, for one).

Born in Chicago, raised in New York City, college-trained in Iowa and California, and made famous in outer space—Koenig, like DeForest Kelley, had flirted with the idea of a medical career (he had even taken the pre-med course at Grinnell in Iowa) before he made his final decision to become an actor.

Walter had his first shot at acting when he was a high school student in New York City's prestigious Fieldston School—one of the Ethical Culture schools. He played the lead in *Peer Gynt* in his sophomore year, then did Shaw's *The Devil's Disciple* in his senior year.

Summer vacations during high school and college were spent setting up a theater program in summer camps for

KOENIG FAN CLUB '75

Walter Koenig's fans are artfully skilled and devoted, as illustrated by this handsome cover. Cover courtesy of the Walter Koenig Official Fan Club from their yearbook.

underpriviledged children and doing summer stock in Vermont.

After two years at Grinnell, Walter switched to UCLA and a psychology major. With his B.A. degree in hand and encouragement from his professor, he headed back to New York to learn the acting craft at the Neighborhood Playhouse. He did so well there that he won a scholarship in his second year. Even so, he had to work hard as a hospital orderly to survive.

At last, jobs began to come Walter's way. He spent two years in Off-Broadway productions, then went back to Los Angeles to do stage and TV roles—among them, the part of Chekov, navigator of the **Enterprise**. The rest is fandom history. Fan mail volume was amazingly heavy, and if the series had continued, more attention would have been focused on this appealing personality, no doubt about that. He was attractive to an important part of the audience and a very competent actor, as well.

His private life is as successful and rewarding as his professional life. He's been happily married to actress

Judy Levitt since 1966. They have two lovely children, Joshua Andrew and Danielle Beth. Northern California is their home.

Facts of Life:

Birthplace: Chicago
Birthday: September 14 (Virgo)
Weight: 130
Height: 5'8''
Hair: Brown
Eyes: Brown

Major acting credits:

Stage: *The Deputy, Night Must Fall*
Movies: *Goodbye, Raggedy Ann*
TV Appearances in *Mr. Novak, Jericho, I Spy, The Alfred Hitchcock Hour, The Lieutenant, The Man from Shiloh, Ironside, Medical Center, Great Adventure, Columbo*

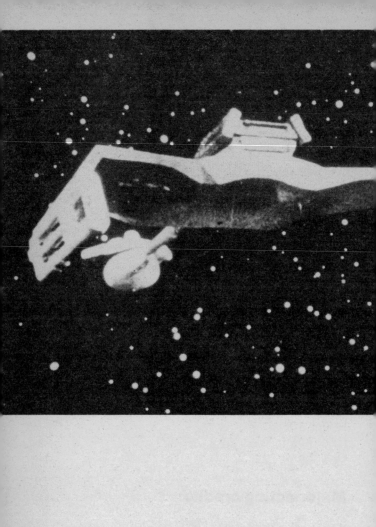

The
Episodes

Introduction

For all the stir the **ST** episodes occasioned on their original telecasts, the real strength of the series is perhaps best observed now, in syndication. Most markets today broadcast episodes on a five-day-a-week basis. In terms of character development alone, this frequency is a godsend: seen only weekly, Lieutenant Uhura may appear to be a one-dimensional piece of cardboard ("Hailing frequencies open, Captain"), as Scotty seems to have but one line ("Captain, the engines just can't take much more!"). The interrelationships between crew members, in particular, are short-changed; only continuity can provide insight into the Spock/McCoy dialogue, for example, or the bond between Kirk and his first officer.

Besides—speaking realistically—television is not by nature a quality medium. Making superior productions week after week after week is probably an impossible task. For all the talent and energy **ST** brought to bear against these facts of creative life, no one would claim that each individual episode is the qualitative equivalent of every other.

So we are more fortunate than we might think. A one-

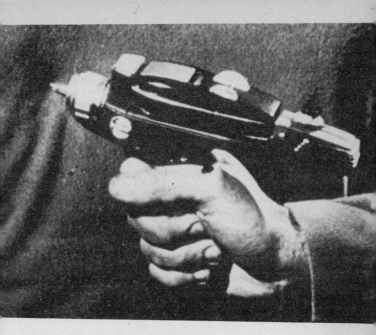

Captain Kirk fell in love
many times but the only
woman he married was
the lovely Miramanee in
"The Paradise Syn-
drome." Artist: Joni
Wagner for Furaha.

Above:
The famous phaser gun
finds itself in the hands of
an alien disguised as a
member of the *Enterprise*
crew. © Paramount Pic-
tures Corporation.

day dip in production values or a single inferior teleplay is only a minor irritant in the present context: it's like the daily, meaningless fluctuations in the stock market—only we're assured of a generally "bull" market! For once, sheer quantity is a boon to overall quality.

It's the ideas expressed in the series that are more clearly focused with frequency. And, after all, the ideas are what count. Seen in succession—on television or in the index that follows—the motivating concepts of Mr. Roddenberry's dream are more inspiring than ever. Furthermore, placing individual episodes into their proper creative context (as S—F, as history) is of primary importance, and one of the goals toward which this index is directed.

Episode 1: The Man Trap

by George Clayton Johnson

There are as many candidates for **the** lead-off episode as there are **ST** fans—or at least **ST** stories. The one that actually did so (and such things are largely a luck-of-the-draw situation) featured a fat part for DeForest Kelley as Dr. McCoy, and one of the best of all **ST** monsters. This one can take human form, and does . . . that of an old girlfriend of McCoy's. (In human form, the actress was Jeanny Bal; the monster, Francine Pyne.) The illusion is far from pretty—in more ways than one—since the alien extracts all salt from human bodies. It's a roundabout way to murder but the effect is the same—as McCoy must discover before it's his turn.

Airdate: 6609.08

Spock's betrothed
T'Pring, played by
Arlene Martel. ©
Paramount Pic-
tures Corporation.

Superman Khan
(Ricardo Mon-
talban) in "Space
Seed." © Para-
mount Pictures
Corporation.

Above:
Robert Walker, Jr., as "Charlie X." © Paramount Pictures Corporation.

Kirk flanked by Mudd's "Alice" series, played by Rhae and Alyce Andrece. © Paramount Pictures Corporation.

Episode 2: Charlie X

by Dorothy Fontana, from a story by Gene Roddenberry

Robert Walker, Jr., guests in the title role, that of an adolescent raised in a world inhabited by noncorporeal beings. His infatuation with his life among humans—and his crush on Yeoman Rand—has a dark side: his immense psychic powers make him a dangerous character when crossed. Kirk is eventually convinced that it was Charlie who was responsible for the destruction of the USS **Antares**, and figures the **Enterprise** is next unless the boy/man can be stopped. This is some powerful puberty, and it's clear that his background has made him unfit—at least during a troubled adolescence—for human contact. A very poignant ending.

Airdate: 6609.15

Episode 3: Where No Man Has Gone Before

by Samuel Peeples

This episode was originally produced as the second pilot for the series, after the first was turned down by NBC for "not enough action." (The first pilot, "The Cage," was later incorporated into a two-part episode, "The Menagerie.") And action this episode is certainly full of! An energy field affects two aboard the **Enterprise**—a woman psychologist as well as one of Kirk's oldest and best friends (played by Gary Lockwood)—giving them violent powers, including telekinesis. Kirk determines that they must be destroyed, but the two have other ideas. The psychologist eventually comes to the Captain's aid before she, too, is killed. (Sally Kellerman, soon to set the world on fire as "Hot Lips" in

Robert Altman's M *A *S *H, turned in a performance as superior as her character's mental powers.)
   Airdate: 6609.22

Episode 4: The Naked Time

by John D. F. Black

Part of the interest—and fun!—of any continuing series is watching characters develop, week by week. Of course, **ST** has its competitors beat not only because its chief characters are intrinsically more interesting than most, but also because its futuristic setting allows for some radical changes as well as gradual development. Kirk alone, at one time or another, goes mad, becomes senile, has his body inhabited by a power-hungry woman—you name it. In this story the entire crew goes on what appears to be an extended acid trip (actually caused by a space disease), with personality changes abounding—Spock a big cry-baby, Nurse Chapel in love with Spock, and so on. Under certain circumstances, the situation might be tolerable for a time, but the **Enterprise** is crashing into a disintegrating planet! McCoy has to find an antidote to the virus . . . and fast.
   Airdate: 6609.29

Episode 5: The Enemy Within

by Richard Matheson

One of the more astute creations made during the construction stage of the series was surely the transporter device. In story-telling terms alone (eliminating excess and-then-he-went-to time), it's invaluable. Besides, the transporter is a universal dream—who wouldn't prefer it, say from Houston to Boston, to a plane trip! It's fortunate, for this plot anyway, that the transporter is not infallible. Here

Kirk is beamed aboard as two separate people: the good Kirk and the bad Kirk, both in danger of dying from the separation. Shatner has a field day.

Airdate: 6610.6

Episode 6: Mudd's Women

by Stephen Kandel, from a story by Gene Roddenberry

Three miners are holding out on much-needed dilithium crystals, and the trade they have in mind is more than Kirk's conscience can take. They want the three beautiful women whom conman Harry Mudd was transporting through space when Kirk arrested him. The source of their beauty: the illegal "Venus drugs." It's an odd story, swinging wildly from comedy to tragedy, but it obviously left its impression. Mudd, as played by Roger C. Carmel, became practically a continuing character, with later appearances on both the live-action and animated series.

Airdate: 6610.13

Episode 7: What Are Little Girls Made Of?

by Robert Bloch

An android is generally defined (though you'd have to get a fairly recent Webster's to find it listed at all) as an automaton—or robot—resembling a human. In this story of the mad Dr. Korby (Michael Strong), his androids are set to take over the **Enterprise**—and Kirk, of course, is a primary candidate for "replacement." Here Nurse Chapel is not yet McCoy's assistant, but rather an old girlfriend of the villain's! Despite this ambivalence, she ends up the heroine. (Other guest stars included Sherry Jackson—didn't she used to be Danny Thomas's daughter?—and, as the gargantuan guard, Ted Cassidy.)

Airdate: 6610.20

Episode 8: Miri

by Adrian Spies

Several times in the series, the producers seem to have looked rather askance at youth; this first-season offering makes the children an anarchic group of vicious beasts. It seems that a fatal disease (first symptoms like leprosy) has killed all the adults and also kills the children as they reach puberty, an event occurring after a life span of hundreds of years. When the **Enterprise** crew beams down, they too begin the disease process, and must find a cure not only for the children but for themselves. Kirk is able to win the trust of only one of the gang of children, Miri (played by Kim Darby, who went on to the film *True Grit*). Also guesting was Michael J. Pollard, who would shortly make an impact in *Bonnie and Clyde*.

Airdate: 6610.27

Episode 9: Dagger of the Mind

by Shimon Wincelberg

People seeing this episode only in syndication may forget that on its initial airing, the story must have had an impact on the then-raging debate over psychosurgery, the radical techniques available for the control of mental patients. On Tantalus V, Dr. Adams, the director of the penal colony there, has devised a "neural neutralizer" to keep his charges in line. For his efforts to fight Dr. Adams, Kirk himself comes due for a little brain readjustment! James Gregory has a high time in the role of the doctor, somewhat similar to that played by the late Charles Laughton in a film version of the H. G. Wells classic *Island of Dr. Moreau*. (The film was released as *The Island of Lost Souls*.)

Airdate: 6611.03

Kirk and McCoy enjoy exotic entertainment on a brief R ÷ R. © Paramount Pictures Corporation.

Episode 10: The Corbomite Maneuver

by Jerry Sohl

A rotating cube, turning on a corner like a giant multi-colored die, shows up in front of the **Enterprise**. Eventually, Kirk orders it destroyed, only to be faced with a larger (in more ways than one) problem. A giant spherical spaceship (the technical crew is rumored to have created the flagship **Fesarius** with Ping Pong balls), over a mile in diameter, locks onto the ship. A voice announces that by destroying the space buoy, the Federation ship has declared its warlike intentions. The verdict: the **Enterprise** and all aboard will be destroyed. Kirk tries a desperate gambit—explaining to the aliens that a substance ("corbomite") that is carried aboard all starships will automatically eliminate any attacker that destroys a Federation vessel. The battle of wits continues, with the source of the alien wit revealed in a surprise ending. (Hint: the surpise is not very tall, and played by Clint Howard.)
   Airdate: 6611.10

Episode 11: The Menagerie

by Gene Roddenberry

The original pilot for the series (entitled "The Cage") was deemed inadequate by the network, and never shown. Here, in the only two-part episode in **ST** history, the footage is used as a flashback within a story that has Spock quite off the wall. He kidnaps Kirk's predecessor, Captain Pike, takes over the **Enterprise**, changes course to an off-limits planet (Talos IV), then turns himself in for court martial! The penalty if convicted: death. It's difficult to see how different the series might have been in its original format from this limited evidence—but it's fun trying. Guest stars include Jeffrey ("thank-your-lucky-stars-Bill-

Shatner") Hunter, Susan Oliver, and Julie Parrish.
Airdates: 6611.17 and .24

Episode 12: The Conscience of the King

by Barry Trivers

This story owes more than its title to Shakespeare's
Hamlet: here too it's a company of actors who are used to
set the trap for the guilty party—in this case, the leader of
the company himself. Kirk should be able to identify a
mass murderer known as "Kodos the Executioner," but he
isn't sure. However, as the other people who could identify
Kodos are picked off one by one, he'd better make up his
mind fast! He's next in line. . . .
Airdate: 6612.08

Episode 13: Balance of Terror

by Paul Schneider

We've seen in our own time the speed with which each
new weapon is made obsolete by a successive technological breakthrough. In this story, the Romulans have developed new weaponry (and tested it on Federation outposts!), as well as a screening device that makes their
ships invisible to Federation sensors. (A similar device
makes an appearance in "The Enterprise Incident,"
Episode 56.) But, technological breakthrough or no, Kirk
orders pursuit. And, as always, the enemy—here the
Romulan commander, played by Mark Lenard—can be as
personally engaging as he is dangerous. (Opticals of the
meter-wide model for the Romulan craft handled by Film
Effects.)
Airdate: 6612.13

Episode 14: Shore Leave

by Theodore Sturgeon

Shades (or premonitions. . .) of *Westworld!* Only the crew of the **Enterprise** fail to be amused by this amusement park where everything you think of comes true. An old school chum torments Kirk, McCoy is apparently killed in battle with a medieval knight, a World War II fighter strafes the crew—even a tiger shows up to make trouble—before Spock begins to unravel the mystery. Eventually, of course, their host makes his appearance, putting out the welcome mat just a bit late. (Locations filmed at Africa USA, near Los Angeles.)
   Airdate: 6612.29

Episode 15: The Galileo Seven

by Oliver Crawford and S. Bar-David

Spock and other crew members set out in the shuttlecraft **Galileo** to investigate the quasar, Murasaki 312. They must set down on a nearby planet for repairs. Unfortunately, Tarus II is occupied by a race of Goliath-like monsters, and no help is possible, since the quasar has knocked out all communications as well as the **Enterprise**'s sensors. This is Spock's first command situation, and he is nearly faced with mutiny. Guesting are Don Marshall, Peter Marko, Grant Woods, and Rees Vaughan. (Note: A monster mask used in this episode, though never for closeups, has reportedly shown up at various conventions.)
   Airdate: 6701.05

Episode 16: The Squire of Gothos

by Paul Schneider

A sort of "Liberace of Space," Trelane is quite the snappy

dresser—velvet waistcoat, lace ruffles at the neck, the works. His behavior is somewhat less laughable, however, as he invites Kirk and crew down to the planet which he inhabits alone, for a banquet . . . and this is one party for which no "regrets" are acceptable. William Campbell plays Trelane (and Liberace!) with plenty of—well, let's say "verve."

Airdate: 6701.12

Episode 17: Arena

by Gene Coon, from a story by Fredric Brown

By and large, **ST** managed to avoid the monster-of-the-week syndrome with which TV tends to infect its S–F offerings. But the crew of the **Enterprise** did have to deal with monsters from time to time, and this week's was one of the best. Reminiscent of the Creature in *Creature from the Black Lagoon,* this is the Gorn—captain of an enemy ship and matched with Kirk for a battle unto death. The battle, forced on both by a third race who want to decide which race (the reptilian or the human) should survive, rages through most of the episode. Excellently scripted, especially for a strictly "action story.

Episode 18: Tomorrow Is Yesterday

by Dorothy Fontana

For those who do (or want to) believe in UFOs, this episode offers an answer: the **Enterprise** itself, through a time-warp, finds itself tracked in the skies above twentieth-century Earth. A pursuing jet is about to be destroyed when Kirk orders the pilot beamed aboard in order to save his life. There seems to be no alternative to keeping the pilot on the **Enterprise**, a virtual prisoner, indefinitely—until Spock's computer discovers that the pilot's son (to be) will play a crucial role in the Earth's space program. Does the alteration of a single incident (or person) change the course of history forever? Kirk must decide, in this excellently crafted story. Good scenes (and great comedy) on the Earth of our own day when the **Enterprise** crew beams down to a top-secret installation to destroy evidence. Roger Perry guests as the **Enterprise**'s surprise visitor, Captain Christopher.

Airdate: 6701.26

Episode 19: Court Martial

by Don Mankiewicz and Stephen Carabatsos

The great Elisha Cook, Jr., perhaps best known as Sidney Greenstreet's gunsel in John Huston's The Maltese Falcon, turns in a typically perfect performance as a lawyer with a reputation for pulling off hopeless cases. He'd better pull this one out of the fire, since his client in the court martial proceedings is none other than Captain James Kirk! Adding (heart) injury to insult, the prosecutor is an old romance of Kirk's (played by Areel Shaw). Kirk is accused of killing a crewman, and the evidence is impressive. (Visually impressive, as the prosecution offers videotapes illustrating Kirk's culpability.) It's helpful to know that episode 20 follows this one, as Kirk's outlook seems pretty bleak. (Another point of interest for movie fans: teleplay co-author Mankiewicz is son of the multi-talented Herman Mankiewicz, whose screenplay credits include Dinner at Eight and Citizen Kane.)

Airdate: 6702.02

Episode 20: The Return of the Archons

by Boris Sobelman, from a story by Gene Roddenberry

This involved story takes on everything from Communism

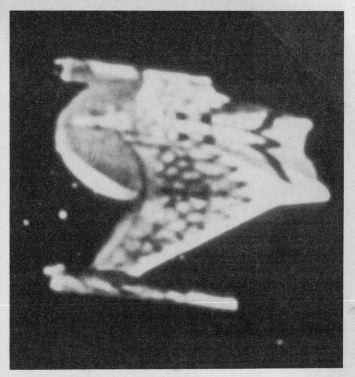

Michael Ansara was one of the many stars who made guest appearances on the series. Still looks like an Indian to me. Photo: David Simons. © Paramount Pictures Corporation.

to organized religion (and points out the similarity between the two), in the context of an exciting plot. The Archons have become a collectivized society of unending sameness, under the dictatorship of a computer, enforcing the teachings of Landru. The crew of the **Enterprise** sets out to encourage the small underground to lead their people to freedom from sixty centuries of oppression.

Airdate: 6702.09

Episode 21: Space Seed

by Gene Coon and Carey Wilbur

Our own immediate future appears during the series only in bits and pieces. Here we learn something of the Eugenics Wars that occupied (or is that "will occupy"?) the last decade of this century. Khan Singh, highly developed creature, held sway over vast areas of Earth—until he was placed in suspended animation on board the SS **Botany Bay**. Discovered by the **Enterprise** and "awakened," Khan has lost none of his strength of will, and loses no time taking over Kirk's ship. Guest stars include Madlyn Rhue and, as Khan, the versatile and talented former Latin Lover of the movies, Ricardo Montalban. (After this appearance, Montalban was featured in sequels to *Planet of the Apes* and, more recently, talking about "crushed velour" and "Corinthian leather" on certain automobile commercials.)

Airdate: 6702.16

Episode 22: A Taste of Armageddon

by Robert Hammer and Gene Coon

What at first appears to be a bloodless computer between the planets Eminar II and Vendikar is found to be quite deadly when the **Enterprise** is counted a "casualty." The rules of the game insist that the crew submit themselves to voluntary extermination, but what seems logical to the planets in the situation is more than Kirk can take. There are stunning special effects in this episode—though a careful study of the background behind the spot where the **Enterprise** crew beams down reveals it to be a matte painting. (Catch the line across the sidewalk in the lower center of the screen; this is where the studio shot has been matched, in the optical printer, with the matte.)

Airdate: 6702.23

Episode 23: This Side of Paradise

by Dorothy Fontana, from a story by Dorothy Fontana and Nathan Butler

As romantic as the F. Scott Fitzgerald novel from which it takes its name, this story has the **Enterprise** crew members falling all over themselves—and Spock falling in love with the beautiful Leila. Their malaise is caused by strange spores encountered on the planet Omicron Ceti III. Quite by accident, Kirk finds a cure—but the crew members are not in the least interested in recovering! Leila is played by Jill Ireland (also known as Mrs. Charles Bronson).

Airdate: 6703.02

Episode 24: Devil in the Dark

by Gene Coon

One of the most serious, and mystifying, questions of space travel is our relationship with life forms different from Earth's. Given our experience with our present environment, it's difficult not to be apprehensive about how we'll treat others. This beauty-*is*-the beast story takes on the question, with an intelligent life form (the Horta) based not on carbon, but silicon. The result: a monster, for all practical—and human—purposes. A strong story, well ex-

Dr. McCoy, Lieutenant Uhura, and Captain Kirk await the arrival of an errant Spock. © Paramount Pictures Corporation.

ecuted. Guest stars include Janos Prohaska, Ken Lynch, Barry Russo, and Brad Weston.

Airdate: 6703.09

Episode 25: Errand of Mercy

by Gene Coon

Placed as they are between the Klingon Empire and the

Federation, the Organians are not really in a position to be
pacifists. Yet that's precisely the attitude they take, despite
Kirk's efforts to warn them against impending Klingon attack. The Organians will not permit any violence, no matter
what the aim (including their own protection). The attack
Kirk feared becomes a reality, but the Organians are not as
helpless as he had thought. Good story, with a guest cast
including John Abbott, John Colicos, Victor Lundin, and
Peter Brocco.
  Airdate: 6703.23

Episode 26: The Alternative Factor

by Don Ingalls

An extension of the idea behind "The Enemy Within" episode (and one that would continue in a second-season story), here it's not Kirk who is divided in half but a space traveler named Lazarus. The stakes are higher here, too, since these two halves must be kept separate. Each is from a different universe, one positive and one negative, with polar-opposite personalities; the sane personality is searching for the insane—but their collision would explode our universe and the other as well. Lazarus is played by Robert Brown.
   Airdate: 6703.30

Episode 27: City on the Edge of Forever

by Harlan Ellison

Is history really just a house of cards: move one—alter a single moment of the past—and the entire structure folds up? The question is an obsession with almost every S–F writer, but has rarely been so interestingly, or tragically, dealt with as in this story, honored by both the Hugo Awards and the Screen Writers Guild. The plot involves the doctor (overdosed on cordrazine), a storefront mission during the Depression of the 1930s, and a woman (Joan Collins guests) who holds the key to future-time, and with whom Kirk falls in love as he and Spock chase McCoy down through history. One of the best.
   Airdate: 6704.06

Episode 28: Operation Annihilate

by Stephen W. Carabatsos

A glimpse, although under painful circumstances, of Kirk's own family; his brother and brother's family live on Deneva. They die there, too—from a parasite that produces pain, madness, then death—and only Kirk's nephew Peter survives. Spock's investigation into a possible cure at first yields only disaster; he himself is attacked by the parasite. But Vulcan control allows him to withstand the pain that makes mere humans insane—and he continues his desperate search. This final episode of the first season featured Craig Hundley as Peter, in addition to Dave Armstrong, Joan Swift, and Maurishka Taliferro.

Airdate: 6704.13.

Episode 29: Amok Time

by Theodore Sturgeon

This was the triumphant premiere of the second season, when Mr. Spock lets his ears down in a most interesting (and informative) episode. Discovered to be quickly losing both his skill and his cool, Spock reveals the secret passion of the Vulcans—bizarre and primitive marriage ritual called Pon Far. It is a rare view of Spock as an emotional being, and a strong picture of the bond between him and Kirk, as the captain is drawn into a lethal battle on Vulcan. His opponent: Spock himself—mad with lust for a betrothed who wants to abandon him. Despite the multilayered fascination of the story, many find it unsettling, after coming to respect the Vulcan mentality, to discover the barbarity of some native customs. The prehistoric ritual in which Kirk and Spock must fight to the death hardly speaks well for Vulcan sophistication. Guest cast includes Arlene Martel (T'Pring) and Celia Lovsky (T'Pau). (Its position in the premiere slot is certainly ironic when one recalls that the network originally thought the Spock character looked "too much like the devil" and might turn off large segments of the audience. The opposite, of course, has proved true.)

Airdate: 6709.15

Episode 30: Who Mourns for Adonis?

by Gilbert Ralston

One of the fruitier of the episodes, here a giant hand—that's right—appears in the middle of space to stop the **Enterprise** in its tracks, or treks. The giant hand belongs to the (sometimes giant) Apollo. Yes, that's **the** Apollo, of Greek mythology fame—who, with his fellow Olympians, turns out to have visited Earth during space travels centuries before. Thus, the magical legends that have come down to us through song and story. Erich von Daniken, meet Edith Hamilton. The plot, which works itself out through the help of a blond lady lieutenant specializing in anthropology, aside—the summation is both interesting and valid: gods exist only when there are worshipers.

Airdate: 6709.22

Episode 31: The Changeling

by John Meredith Lucas

One of the most thoughtful, provocative episodes of the series, the theme is the aftermath of man's creation, in the tale of a "perfect" probe computer sent out from Earth years before. When the **Enterprise** meets up with it, damage during its travels has fatally altered its instructions. The Nomad, instead of seeking out life as originally programmed, has begun to seek out—and "sterilize" or murder—imperfect life. Perilously, such life forms include

Top:
"Who Mourns for Adonis?" features an omnipotent Apollo and the lovely crew member he takes for his consort. © Paramount Pictures Corporation.

A meeting of intergalactic heads of state brings out a variety of beings. © Paramount Pictures Corporation.

the crew of the starship **Enterprise**. They buy time through a fortuitous mistaken identity: Nomad's inventor was a brilliant Earth scientist named Jackson Roykirk, and the deadly computer mistakes Captain James Kirk for its "Creator." When Kirk accidentally identifies himself as a "biological specimen," Nomad decides on a final solution to the imperfection problem and attaches itself to the ship's life support system. The crew of the **Enterprise**, will suffocate. Worse, Nomad gets from the ship's computer the exact location of Earth. If it is allowed to return "home," it will continue its search-and-destroy mission there.

In an interesting denouement, Kirk unhinges the machine by revealing he is not the "Creator." Nomad has made a mistake; Nomad is imperfect and therefore must be "sterilized." They transport the confused computer into space, just before it blows itself up.

Airdate: 6709.29

Episode 32: Mirror, Mirror

by Jerome Bixby

With Spock at the controls, the transporter has a near-fatal malfunction, beaming aboard four crewmen (Kirk, McCoy, Scott, Uhura) who are not quite as they appear. Instead, they are the alternate-universe counterparts to the four; our own beloved crew members have appeared in the alternate-world **Enterprise**. "Alternate" is not a strong enough word; this parallel to our own world is a violent, terror-ridden society. Advancement in the starship service has nothing to do with competence; one moves up the ladder of rank by murdering the "rung" above. Spock is challenged by the switch. He must get the alternate four off his **Enterprise** in a hurry—and find the "real" ones at the same time. (One advantage to the parallel universe: Barbara Luna, guesting as "Marlene.")

Airdate: 6710.06

Episode 33: The Apple.

by Max Ehrlich and Gene Coon, from a story by Max Ehrlich

New sets on a weekly basis are a tough order; though the **ST** people did their best, the "stone" head of Vaal in this episode bears an unfortunate resemblance to papier-mache. The story survives the problem, however, with the endlessly intriguing theme of the loss of innocence (it's the apple of Eden that the title refers to). Vaal sees to all needs of the population on Gamma Trianguli VI. They're immortal, not to mention lazy, mentally stunted, and completely nonproductive. Playing the role of the "snake," as it were, Kirk sees his duty clearly: destroy the machine Vaal and give the locals a chance to lead realistic lives. Naturally, Vaal fights back, causing the **Enterprise**'s orbit to decay.

Airdate: 67.10.13

Episode 34: The Doomsday Machine

by Norman Spinrad

Within a decade after this episode was first aired, *Space: 1999* was to use a similar device for one of its stories: a ship graveyard—a sort of Bermuda Triangle on wheels, sucking in wayward craft. In this story, Kirk reminds us of the antecedents of the "doomsday machine." It's a weapon built primarily as a bluff. It's never meant to be used—so strong it could destroy both sides in a war. Something like the old H-Bomb was supposed to be. . . . Here the machine has continued to operate beyond whatever its original purpose may have been. (Who is to say the H-bomb will not?) There are super visuals of the machine itself—a vast, roughly cylindrical thing like a "space Hoover." William Windom guests as Commodore Decker, who, over-

An artistic rendering of Kirk's transformation into Janet Lister. Artist: Joni Wagner for Furaha.

Akuta and his people must learn to live without the control of Vaal in "The Apple." © Paramount Pictures Corporation.

come with guilt after a previous command failure, takes valiant (if suicidal) action.

Airdate: 6710.20

Episode 35: Catspaw

by Robert Bloch and D.C. Fontana

What seems to be voodoo that first heats the **Enterprise** up to an extremely high temperature and then encases it like a fly in amber, and a giant black cat—these are the two elements of one of the most "supernatural" of all **ST** episodes. The ending is almost inexcusably sad, when we see the witches in their true pitiful forms. But on the way there, keep your eye on the magic wand. The National Air and Space Museum in Washington, D.C., has the tiny, pendantlike model of the **Enterprise** used in this episode in its collection. (Ask for it, maybe they'll finally put it on display!)

Airdate: 6710.27

Episode 36: I, Mudd

by Stephen Kandel

Can the irrepressible Harry Mudd really have met his end when sent off to prison? (See "Mudd's Women," Episode 6.) Did Batman ever completely rid himself of the Joker? Or Superman of Luthor? No, evil (like hope) springs eternal—as do its more personable practitioners. Harcourt Fenton Mudd, who was to appear once again in the animated series, here has found himself the ideal setup. Powerful androids—the women in particular modeled to his exacting specifications—have proclaimed him Mudd I, and follow his every order. His latest instructions: capture the **Enterprise**! The crew manages to overpower the robots only when they hit on the idea of short-circuiting their insistent logic. Perhaps Kirk had plenty of experience, dealing with Spock? (Roger C. Carmel again assays the role of Mudd.)

Airdate: 6711.03

Episode 37: Metamorphosis

by Gene L. Coon

A beautiful and touching story—of love (however "abnormal") and loneliness. Kirk, Spock, McCoy, and a young woman diplomat for whom they are trying to get medical help are forced to land on a supposedly empty planet. There they discover a stranded space pioneer, who's been on the planet for more than two hundred years, kept alive by a powerful (and intelligent) "electric cloud" called the Companion. Since Zephram Cochran is dying (literally) of loneliness, the Companion decides to provide some human company—from the **Enterprise**. The only problem is that Nancy Hedford is dying. A lovely ending. (Cochran is played by Glenn Corbett, Nancy Hedford by Elinor Donahue—late of the *Father Knows Best* series.)

Airdate: 6711.10

Episode 38: Journey to Babel

by Dorothy Fontana

A conference is called to decide the thorny question of Coridan's admission into the Federation, and the **Enterprise** is given the task of transporting the bitterly divided delegates. One is murdered, and the finger of guilt points squarely at the Vulcan ambassador—who is none other than Spock's estranged father! Accompanied by his wife (an Earthwoman), the Vulcan is seriously ill, and only a delicate operation (with Spock providing the blood) can save him. A near-fatal attack on Kirk, an alien spy, a mys-

Glen Corbett and
Elinor Donahue in
"Metamorphosis."
© Paramount Pictures
Corporation.

Right:
"The Deadly Years."
Here, DeForest Kelley
has been transformed
into an effectively ancient
Dr. McCoy. © Paramount
Pictures Corporation.

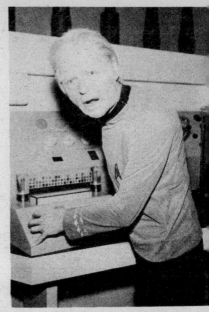

The progressive aging of
James T. Kirk in "The
Deadly Years." © Para-
mount Pictures Corpo-
ration.

tery ship trailing the **Enterprise**—the plot is, to say the least, full. But it works, and excitingly so. (With the preceding episode, this makes for Old Home Fortnight for the *Father Knows Best* crew: Jane Wyatt, who appears here as Spock's mother, Amanda, played Margaret on the old series. Another tidbit for sharp-eyed fans—Mark Lenard, who guests as Spock's father in this episode, was the Romulan commander in Episode 13.)

Airdate: 6711.17

Episode 39: Friday's Child

by Dorothy Fontana

On Capella IV, the Klingons stir up trouble by encouraging a sympathizer to challenge the Teer (or chief) for leadership. According to custom, the widow of a deposed Teer must sacrifice her life—in this case also sacrificing her unborn child. These developments do not go unnoticed by the **Enterprise** crew, who are observing from the planet's surface. When the pregnant Eleen (played by the statuesque Julie Newmar) plans to carry out the custom, Kirk, Spock, and McCoy kidnap her and provide her protection —against her will. Also appearing in the episode: Tige Andrews, Michael Dante, and Cal Bolder.

Airdate: 6712.01

Episode 40: The Deadly Years

by David Harmon

Kirk loses command of the **Enterprise**—not to mention much of his sense—when senility sets in on all exposed crewmen, except one. Chekov is inexplicably unaffected. Commodore Stocker (Charles Drake) assumes command, rushing the afflicted crew through Romulan territory toward medical help. Because of his Vulcan longevity, Spock retains more of his intelligence than the others. His efforts to isolate the problem are compounded by pursuing Romulans. (Shots of Romulan craft utilize old footage from "Balance of Terror.")

Airdate: 6712.08

Episode 41: Obsession

by Art Wallace

A sentient cloud begins to pick off crew members in a fashion disturbingly familiar to Kirk: enveloping a human for a few seconds, the cloud leeches all the red blood cells from its victim's body. The same phenomenon had killed several in the crew of the USS **Farragut** some years before—when Kirk was aboard as a junior officer. Kirk continues to feel guilt for his own inability to have acted more quickly then. He's determined to even the score, the obsession referred to in the title. The process is made more difficult, however, by the fact that the son of the **Farragut** captain, who was among the dead from the first attack, now serves aboard the **Enterprise**. (Actor Stephen Brooks plays the son of the dead Captain Garrovick.)

Airdate: 6712.15

Episode 42: Wolf in the Fold

by Robert Bloch

An R & R break for the **Enterprise** crew on a planet where violence has been abolished almost turns into a violent end for Mr. Scott. First one, then another, brutal murder occurs, with Scott the prime suspect. The trail of death continues, this time with that of the high priestess of the planet, stabbed in Scott's arms. During the investigation, the finger of guilt finally points away from Scott, to the local Federation representative. But he too is a red herring: he is only possessed by the spirit of none other than the famous Jack the Ripper. The spirit is free to pass into any body it chooses—*The Exorcist* has nothing on this plot! McCoy solves the problem by injecting all aboard with a (potent) tranquilizer. Unable to produce violence, the spirit is tricked into the transporter and its molecules are scattered all over space. The happy ending is particularly pleasant for the stoned-to-the-teeth crew; they have a few hours of high times left on the drug!

Airdate: 6712.22

Episode 43: The Trouble with Tribbles

by David Gerrold

No, it just **seems** like this show plays on TV weekly. For a variety of reasons, this simple story has become one of the most familiar of all **ST** episodes, and the creature called a tribble has become recognizable world-wide. The furry little reproduction machines made further appearances (only some of their habits were changed) in the animated **ST** episode "More Troubles, More Tribbles." In addition, author Gerrold wrote a couple of books telling the inside story of the making of this live-action episode, the making of the tribbles, and his own life aboard the **Enterprise**. The plot here, involving a new grain hybrid and an uppity Federation official, is quite secondary to the little fur creatures themselves.

Airdate: 6712.29

Episode 44: The Gamesters of Triskelion

by Margaret Armen

Among the more thoughtful dramatic presentations of slavery to be found anywhere—and no less exciting for its thoughtfulness. The gamesters on Triskelion, also known as the Providers, have developed their mental civilization completely at the expense of the physical. (Kirk is given a glimpse of their physical being: three food-dyed brains sitting under a transparent hemisphere.) They amuse themselves with a group of gladiator-slaves (the Thralls). Kirk, Uhura, and Chekov are slated to become part of the troupe. Of course the Providers have neglected to take into account the gambling instincts of James T. Kirk.

Airdate: 6801.05

Episode 45: A Piece of the Action

by David Harmon and Gene Coon

Anthropologists should stay awake nights worrying after a glance at this episode. A crewman from the USS **Horizon** leaves behind a book about Earth's Chicago gangs of the thirties' era, on the planet Iotia. A century passes, then the **Enterprise** arrives to find that the locals have taken the book quite to heart. An only semi-serious story, it features some funny shots of Mr. Spock in garb à la Al Capone (the ears touch the hat) and some good guest performances. The cast includes Anthony Caruso as the Boss; also Victor Tayback, Lee Delano, John Harmon, Sheldon Collins, Steve Arnold.

Airdate: 6801.12

Episode 46: The Immunity Syndrome

by Robert Sabaroff

Spock is the first to know it, when he senses the death of some 400 Vulcans aboard the ship **Intrepid**. On orders to investigate, the **Enterprise** finds the sister ship has disappeared, along with the entire Gamma 7A star system. In its place is a black void that quickly envelops the **Enterprise** as it is pulled relentlessly to a giant amoeba, a single living cell stretching over thousands of cubic miles of space. In a very well-structured countdown, Spock takes a probe into the middle of the creature, aiming for its nucleus. His power failing, he is able only to report worse news: the cell's chromosomes are lined up for reproduction. Their enemy will soon be plural. The **Enterprise** itself follows Spock's craft into the interior of the cell. Excellent visuals (credit Frank Van Der Veer), and an equally authoritative denouement.

Airdate: 6801.19

Episode 47: A Private Little War

by Gene Roddenberry, from a story by Judd Crucis

On a peaceful planet Kirk had helped explore some years before, the crew finds that gunpowder has suddenly made an appearance. When a Klingon craft is discovered in the area, the logical presumption is that they have armed one group at the expense of another. Kirk is on the scene, trying to contact his old friend Tyree (Michael Whitney), when he is attacked by one of the local beasts, the Mugatu (not one of the series' better-costumed monsters, unfortunately). Kirk is cured by the witch-doctor wife of Tyree, Nona, (played by Nancy Kovack), only to fall under her spell. Reluctantly, he decides to give rifles to Tyree's side of the conflict—but that's not enough for Nona, who wants phasers! There is a really poignant ending to this all-too-familiar tale of war, and the supposed instincts for war.

Airdate: 6802.02

Episode 48: Return to Tomorrow

by John Kingsbridge

Three beings are in search of human bodies to house

them while they construct androids for themselves. Their search seems ended when they find Kirk, Spock, and a doctor aboard the **Enterprise** (guesting, Diana Muldaur). A good story, but most memorable is a speech of Kirk's: "Men used to say that if man could fly, he'd have wings. But he did fly; he discovered he had to. Do you wish that the first Apollo mission hadn't reached the moon? Or that we hadn't gone on to Mars, and then to the nearest star? . . . Risk—risk is our business. That's what this starship is all about. That's why we are aboard her." It could be the **ST** motto.

Airdate: 6802.09

Episode 49: Patterns of Force

by John Meredyth Lucas

A scarifying story, wherein the **Enterprise** crew members discover a culture based on German National Socialism—complete with swastikas and the SS. The "Jews" of the piece are the neighboring (and minority) Zeons. There's even a "Führer," and he is—or was—a Federation sociologist (played by David Brian). Some experiment! This episode is not easy to take, even when one knows that in fifty-three minutes it will be "up and out," with Kirk and crew having set the situation to rights. And William Shatner may regret the plethora of stills around featuring him disguised in an SS uniform!

Airdate: 6802.16

Episode 50: By Any Other Name

by Dorothy Fontana and Jerome Bixby, from a story by Jerome Bixby

Answering a distress call on a supposedly uninhabited planet, the crew and ship are overpowered by aliens who

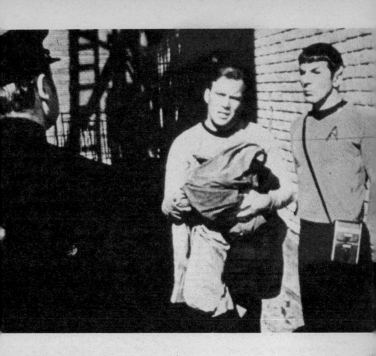

Above:
Kirk and Spock try to rationalize their situation to a twentieth-century policeman in this scene from "City on the Edge of Forever."

In "Patterns of Force," Kirk and McCoy don Nazi uniforms in an attempt to foil a self-styled Fuhrer. © Paramount Pictures Corporation.

have taken human form. From the Kelvin Empire in the Andromeda galaxy, Rojan (Warren Stevens) and his followers commandeer the **Enterprise** for the intergalactic return to their world. They have entered our galaxy searching for a new world to inhabit ("We do not colonize, we conquer," Rojan informs Kirk), looking toward the day when their own empire is uninhabitable. Kirk tries everything—including serious consideration of blowing up the ship—until they hit on the idea of exploiting the unfamiliarity of the Kelvins with their new human bodies, and their senses. (Guess who's elected to stimulate the romantic senses of Kelinda, played by Barbara Bouchet?)

Airdate: 6802.23

Episode 51: The Omega Glory

by Gene Roddenberry

A story of perhaps greater impact during our Bicentennial year than when first aired. The moral is simple: documents of freedom and liberty are just that—documents—without constant practice of their stated virtues. Here, the descendants of the capitalist-versus-Communist struggle of our own day have transferred their argument to another planet. On Omega IV, both cultures have deteriorated to the point where treasured documents (like the U.S. Constitution) are worshiped as relics, not as ideals. Kirk is determined to set them right. Guesting are Morgan Woodword, Roy Jensen, Irene Kelley, David L. Ross, Ed McReady, Lloyd Kino, Morgan Farley.

Airdate: 6803.01

Episode 52: The Ultimate Computer

by D. C. Fontana, from a story by Lawrence N. Wolfe

An underlying dream of the technological era—a computer that can "think"—has become a reality in this story, and the war games in which it's being tested are a deadly reality! A constant theme of modern science fiction, going back at least as far as Mary Shelley's *Frankenstein*, has been the machine that turns upon its masters. Here, the M-5 does just that, attacking other Federation craft and killing dozens. Kirk averts the ultimate disaster with some shrewd second-guessing, including a suicide suggestion to the computer reminiscent of "The Changeling" episode. William Marshall plays Daystrom, inventor of the M-5.

Airdate: 6803.08

Episode 53: Bread and Circuses

by Gene Roddenberry and Gene Coon, from a story by John Kneubuhl

A TV game show called **Name the Winner** where gladiators fight it out Roman-style? (Are you listening, Chuck "Gong Show" Barris?) Well, it hasn't happened yet, but you never know. The defrocked captain of the starship **Beagle** (Merik, played by William Smithers) has this bright idea to entertain the subjects of the dictatorship modeled after that of Imperial Rome. When Kirk and other crewmen refuse to join Merik, they find the only alternative is a television "guest appearance."

Airdate: 6803.15

Episode 54: Assignment Earth

by Gene Roddenberry, from a story by Gene Roddenberry and Art Wallace

This episode was the pilot for a Roddenberry series that never got off the ground—the story of a human named Gary Seven (played by Robert Lansing) who has been raised by aliens and sent to Earth to prevent nuclear disaster. Thus, the **Enterprise** shows up on the Earth of our own day (1968, to be exact). In this unsold pilot, however, it's unclear to Kirk (and the audience) whether Seven is a force for good or evil. A gripping story: who knows where it might have gone as a series? (Gene Roddenberry probably did, but the network didn't seem too anxious to ask the question.) Episode includes footage of the Saturn V launching from Cape Kennedy and guest stars Terri Garr, Don Keefer, and Isis (the cat).

Airdate: 6803.29

Episode 55: Spock's Brain

by Lee Cronin

A beautiful apparition emerges on the **Enterprise**, and when she disappears, so has Spock's brain! Dr. McCoy manages to keep Spock's body alive and walking mechanically, but it can only be temporary. Racing against time, Kirk and McCoy—accompanied by the zombied Spock— beam down to the planet. There they find a double world. On the surface is a race of Neanderthal-like men; below are a highly advanced technology and a bevy of beauties who seem quite as brainless as poor Spock. Who is responsible for this "advanced" culture? The women speak of the "Controller," but no such person is to be found. What's more, Spock's disembodied voice can be heard, although he has no idea where his brain resides—or why it was removed. Guest stars for this premiere episode of the final (to date!) season were Marj Dusay, Sheila Leighton, and James Daris.

Airdate: 6809.20

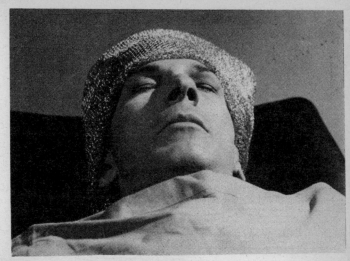

Top:
A somewhat incapacitated Mr. Spock in "Spock's Brain." © Paramount Pictures Corporation.

Bottom:
Renowned attorney Melvin Belli, as Gorgon, gave a satisfyingly menacing performance in "And the Children Shall Lead." © Paramount Pictures Corporation.

Episode 56: The Enterprise Incident

by Dorothy Fontana

Kirk makes a seemingly foolish error in crossing Romulan barriers, only to have the **Enterprise** captured. What a feather in the cap of the Romulan commander (a beautiful performance from the beautiful Joanne Linville)—particularly since Spock implies he might join forces with her. Have Kirk and Spock gone mad—the one stupid and the other a traitor? The obvious answer is "no," but few things are quite as apparent as they seem (and that includes the Romulan craft, with their new cloaking device) in this twisted plot. The Romulan vessels were actually the new 29-inch miniatures designed by Matt Jeffries for the Klingons. It's a fact of TV life that scripts rarely appear on the screen in their original written form. There's a standard assumption that all such cases represent, at the least, a dilution of superior material; this cannot always be the case—sometimes what is superior on paper can quite easily be inferior on film. Here, however, the cliché[1] holds true, and the original teleplay is worth looking for.)

Airdate: 6809.27

Episode 57: The Paradise Syndrome

by Margaret Armen

An asteroid rushes toward an unfamiliar planet; beaming down, the crew find a civilization indistinguishable from that of the more advanced American Indian tribes. Their numbers are so few that evacuation is no problem—until Kirk disappears inside a strange obelisk obviously constructed by an outside culture. By the time Kirk reappears, the **Enterprise** is gone (off to try to deflect the asteroid), along with his memory. For the natives, however, he's the god that the builders of the obelisk had promised them.

William Shatner seems to enjoy his release from the constraints of his usual role, and turns in an outstanding performance.

Airdate: 6810.04

Episode 58: And the Children Shall Lead

by Edward J. Lasko

Beaming down to a planet in distress, the crew finds that a wave of mass suicide has decimated its population. The survivors: five children. Back on the ship, the less-than-blessed children seem to have some very odd games—right out of *Lord of the Flies*. They can summon a guiding spirit, played by Melvin Belli. The children are capable of influencing others, and were responsible for the deaths of their own parents. Guided by the Gorgon, they are setting out to use the same powers on the **Enterprise** crew, then throughout the galaxy, until Kirk can discredit the Gorgon —and touch their own feelings of guilt and sadness.

Airdate: 6810.11

Episode 59: Is There In Truth No Beauty?

by Jean Lisette Aroeste

A subtly touching story of the Medusan ambassador, who comes aboard with his beautiful, uh, "assistant." You see, the ambassador is of a race that, like the Greek horror from which it took its name, no human may look upon without disastrous consequences. His doctor companion is essential for his dealings with humans; in addition, she, a human, still seems able to look at him without harmful effects. Spock too, with special glasses, appears to have some immunity, though it's sorely tested at the end of the episode

Above:
Spock's parents meet the
Enterprise officers.
Photo: David Simons.
© Paramount Pictures
Corporation.

Jane Wyman portrayed
the lovely and gracious
human mother of Mr.
Spock. © Paramount Pic-
tures Corporation.

when he must attempt a mind fusion with the Medusan. Diana Muldaur guest-stars as the interpreter, Miranda.
   Airdate: 6810.18

Episode 60: Spectre of the Gun

by Lee Cronin

At first glance the old "time machine" gambit again, this episode only seems to have transported Kirk, Spock, et al., to a reenactment of the famed "Gunfight at the O.K. Corral." In reality, it's the punishment of Milkotians, but the **Enterprise** crew can be forgiven its concern: they're cast as the Clanton gang, the victims! The "High Noon" quality of the plotting, as the minutes tick away to the appointed hour, gives the tale more than average interest, as does Spock's final solution to their dilemma. Put simply: if **they** know the whole scene to be an illusion, then the bullets must be equally imaginary. It remains only for them to keep this disbelief firmly in mind; not an easy task, but then the crew members are a match for it.
   Airdate: 6810.25

Episode 61: Day of the Dove

by Jerome Bixby

Michael Ansara and Susan Howard guest in a violent episode about the futility of violence. First the **Enterprise** crewmen are at one another's throats; then suddenly Klingons are aboard. Obviously, some sort of game has been set in motion—both sides are armed only with swords, and even fatal wounds heal amost immediately. But this "game" would appear to have no end: unending murder aboard the **Enterprise**, no release even in death (which has apparently been abolished to keep things interesting). Kirk figures the glowing "thing" that draws energy from the violence can be contained only if all hatred is brought under control. Convincing the Klingon leader Kang of this is, however, another matter.

Airdate: 6811.01

Episode 62: For the World Is Hollow, and I Have Touched the Sky

by Rik Vollaerts

McCoy's prognosis of his disease is that he has only a year to live. (Could DeForest Kelley have been talking to the NBC executives about the impending cancellation?) This interesting story—with its beautiful title—tells of the "world" of Yonada, set on a collision course with Daran V. What the locals don't know is that theirs is not a planet at all; it's an enormous spacecraft inside a hollow sphere, sent into space by ancestors of ten millenia before when the Fabrini solar system was about to die. Ruled by a computer-engine (the Oracle) through an "instrument of obedience" placed just under the skin at the temple, the citizens of Yonada are allowed no questions, no doubts. Kirk wants to avert disaster without destroying the "planet," but the high priestess Natira (Kate Woodville) forbids anything approaching blasphemy. However, McCoy has a special way with the lady—she proposes to him, and it appears he will accept—and her Oracle holds the secret to his cure.

Airdate: 6811.08

Episode 63: The Tholian Web

by Judy Burns and Chet Richards

Mutiny is hardly a regular occurrence in the Starfleet, but that's what appears to have happened aboard the USS **Defiance**; four of the **Enterprise** crew beam aboard to find that everyone on the ship has murdered everyone else. To make matters worse, the ship and all aboard are disintegrating. Transporter troubles on the **Enterprise** make it possible to beam only three crewmen back—Kirk elects to remain, and the rest of the episode is occupied with trying to snatch his apparitionlike body from open space. The alien Tholians show up to put a ringer in the effort, as their craft spins a sort of "spider web" around the helpless **Enterprise**. Frank Van Der Veer gets credit for the superb optical work.

Airdate: 6811.15

Episode 64: Plato's Stepchildren

by Meyer Dolinsky

The ideals of Ancient Greece seem to have had less effect on this civilization than have the fashions. More crucial to their mean-spirited lifestyle is their ability in telekinesis— the "mind over matter" concept more recently explored in Brian de Palma's film *Carrie*. Guest-starring is the late Michael Dunn (of Broadway theater roles, including *The Ballad of the Sad Cafe,* and films, including *Ship of Fools*), a great actor and great human being, who was only incidentally short in stature.

Airdate: 6811.22

Episode 65: Wink of an Eye

by Lee Cronin

An interesting and well-handled story of survival, where the only clues are the story of a dead civilization and a strange buzzing sound in the ears of the **Enterprise** crew. Could there be insects aboard? Probably not, but there is a visitor—a machine that appears, attaching itself to the ship's life support system. Stumped, Kirk's knowledge is increased—along with his metabolism—by a drugged cup of coffee. His life systems are speeded up to the level of the Scalosians, who have boarded the **Enterprise**. Thus the buzzing: it's the voices of the aliens, their metabolisms super-charged to the point where they are invisible to slow-moving humans. Their machine is a refrigeration device to put the crew into suspended animation, from which —one by one—the men can be recharged and used for stud services in place of the sterile alien males. Kirk is among the first to be so chosen (naturally), and by the beautiful alien leader (again, naturally!). He cleverly manages to communicate with the sluggish Spock, and save the ship. Excellent handling of slow-motion photography.

Airdate: 6811.29

Episode 66: The Empath

by Joyce Muskat

Visiting a planet whose sun is about to nova, Kirk, Spock, and McCoy find no trace of the previous inhabitants. Instead, they find themselves beamed below the surface of the planet where awaits a beautiful, though mute, woman. She is an unwilling participant in a "research" endeavor run by two aliens, Lal and Thann, into which the **Enterprise** crew is drawn. Sadistic torture scenes are relieved (in both senses) by the lovely Gem (Kathryn Hays), who is capable of empathetic cures—though at great cost to her own system.

Airdate: 6812.06

Episode 67: Elaan of Troyius

by John M. Lucas

The fabulously beautiful Elaan, who is practically a god to her people, has become a pawn to her power: she must marry the chief of Troyius—her people's historical ene-

Top:
The "mail-order" bride episode linked Mr. Spock with the beautifully bedecked Susan Danberg. Photo: Wide World.

In "Elaan of Troyius," France Nuyen captures Kirk's adoration with her irresistible love tears. © Paramount Pictures Corporation.

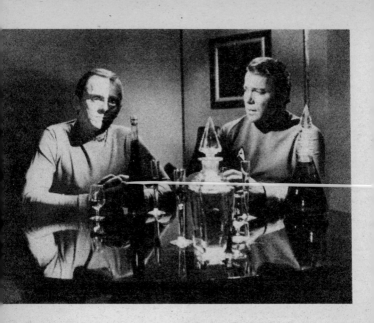

Impressionist Frank Gorshin in a change-of-pace role in "Let That Be Your Last Battlefield," a futuristic examination of racial prejudice. © Paramount Pictures Corporation.

Right:
Julie Newmar guest-starred as Eleen in "Friday's Child." © Paramount Pictures Corporation.

mies. And guess who's elected to transport the raging priestess to her fate? Captain James Kirk, who at least can sympathize with her about the burdens of responsibility. She's like a violent Amazon, however—or Katherine in *The Taming of the Shrew*—and not about to give up without a fight. France Nuyen turns in a memorable guest performance as Elaan (though admittedly Ms. Nuyen could easily be memorable reading stock quotations). Other guests include Jay Robinson, Tony Young, Lee Duncan, and Victor Brandt.

Airdate: 6812.20

Episode 68: Whom Gods Destroy

by Lee Erwin

A Federation insane asylum erupts in violent rebellion, while Kirk and Spock are drawn into the battle. The leader of the revolt, Garth, has an advantage over the **Enterprise** crew: he can alter his form at will. And his goals don't stop with control of the asylum—he plans to lead his followers into intergalactic conquest. The vehicle for their invasion is, naturally, the **Enterprise**. Appearing in the episode are Steve Ihnat (Garth), Yvonne Craig, and Keye Luke.

Airdate: 6901.03

Episode 69: Let That Be Your Last Battlefield

by Oliver Crawford, from a story by Lee Cronin

That tired old *The Defiant Ones* cliché is played out, S–F style, in this indictment of racial (or more specifically, simple color) prejudice. Two aliens are each split right down the middle—half black shoe polish, half white but on opposite sides—and one chases after the other, the "different" one, without a thought for the similarities. Frank

Gorshin plays the baddie (his routine James Cagney impression comes in handy for the part), and Lou Antonio the oppressed figure.

Airdate: 6901.10

Episode 70: The Mark of Gideon

by George F. Slavin and Stanley Adams

Kirk is to be the first outsider visiting the Garden-of-Eden planet of Gideon—but the transporter sends him instead to a duplicate **Enterprise**, with no one else aboard! No one, that is, except Odona (Sharon Acker), and she claims to know nothing of how she got there either, or even from where she came. Some chilling scenes in this episode (odd glimpses through the false **Enterprise**'s viewscreens), and some unsettling thoughts on overpopulation, longevity, and the "conquest" of disease. Joining Ms. Acker in the guest cast are David Hurst, Gene Kynarski, and Richard Derr.

Airdate: 6901.17

Episode 71: That Which Survives

by John M. Lucas, from a story by Dorothy Fontana

A fairly extreme version of all those lethal lovelies of whom Raymond Chandler and Ian Fleming so often wrote—and who've made their share of **ST** appearances—occupies center stage in this story, a version with a twist. Losira can kill with a touch, literally, but there's a method to her meanness. The **Enterprise** officers discover her on a planet that couldn't possibly support life—no plants, no water—and her very existence is as surprising as her comings and goings. (In an excellent visual effect, she pulls herself into a hair-thin line, then draws up to a point.) Lee

Meriwether guests as Losira, joined by Arthur Batanides and Naomi Pollack.

Airdate: 6901.24

Episode 72: The Lights of Zetar

by Jeremy Tarcher and Shari Lewis

Scott is sweet on a new **Enterprise** female crew member, but what at first seems a matter of her "getting her space legs" becomes considerably more serious. Lieutenant Mira Romaine is oddly affected by a strange phenomenon (visualized as clustered lights) trailing the ship, to the point where she anticipates alien actions—and attacks on the phenomenon come close to killing her. The most unsettling of her premonitions: the death of Mr. Scott! In an investigation, McCoy and Spock discover that her brain waves have been altered—duplicating the energy patterns of the alien force. Not an "it" at all, this is a "them," a race searching through space for a body to occupy. They have picked Lieutenant Romaine as their target, but Kirk and Scott make it a battleground as they encourage her to resist. (Mira Romaine is played by Jan Shutan.)

Airdate: 6901.31

Episode 73: Requiem for Methuselah

by Jerome Bixby

In the Book of Genesis, "all the days of Methuselah were nine hundred sixty and nine years"; then, in the Bible's succinct way of handling these matters, "he died." Author Bixby suggests that he didn't die at all, but rather went on cropping up as one historical figure after another (King Solomon at one point and later, forsaking biblical personages for artistic, Leonardo da Vinci). Now he is Flint and, as played by James Daly, lives in seclusion from the universe with a single companion, his charge Reena (Louise Sorel). Discovered by the **Enterprise**, he would have the entire crew die rather than have his whereabouts revealed. Reena is more pleased to receive visitors—with a special invitation to Kirk.

Airdate: 6902.14

Episode 74: This Way to Eden

by Arthur Heinemann, from a story by Arthur Heinemann and Michael Richards

Considering the historical moment of its initial screening— just a month after the first Nixon inauguration—the political implications of this tale of mad "hippies" from the twenty-third century may be somewhat hard to take. But such considerations aside, this story doesn't offer much in the way of lasting interest—certainly not its original "rocket rock" song ("Hey, Out There" by Charles Napier, who also guest-stars in the episode). The craft **Aurora** may be recognized as the Tholian "spider ship" from Episode 63; a model has been donated by Richard Van Treuren to the National Air and Space Museum in Washington, D.C.

Airdate: 6902.21

Episode 75: The Cloud Minders

by Margaret Armen, from a story by David Gerrold and Oliver Crawford

Similar to Fritz Lang's *Metropolis:* the subterranean working-class slaves to provide the luxury required by the leisure class above. Here, the lower world is on the surface of the planet, while the masters reside in the cloud city Ardana. Zeenite is the principal product of the working-class miners—and Kirk must get his hands on a shipment. To do so, however, he (with Spock and McCoy) become

involved in a budding revolution. Guesting, Fred William-
son.
   Airdate: 6902.28

Episode 76: The Savage Curtain

**by Arthur Helnemann and Gene Roddenberry, from a
story by Gene Roddenberry**

It's clear—even from this brief glance at the episodes—
that the stories in which Roddenberry is personally involved tend to be heavy with ideas. This doesn't mean
"heaviness" necessarily, for a strong story can always
carry a full load of thought; after all, that's what fiction is all
about. Here, however, Kirk and Spock join forces with Abe
Lincoln and the father of Vulcan philosophy in a battle
against four representatives of evil (Genghis Khan is one).
And it doesn't come off. Speechifying is relieved only by
another round of violence—but there's plenty of that for
those who like it. Honest Abe is played by Lee Bergere,
Genghis by Nathan Jung.
   Airdate: 6903.07

Episode 77: All Our Yesterdays

by Jean Lisette Aroeste

A fairly standard "time portals" story takes on more-than-
standard interest as Spock evidences some mild romantic
interest, while Kirk is almost burned as a witch. On a
doomed planet, the locals have disappeared—except the
librarian (and his android duplicates) of a very strange library. All the inhabitants have been transported to the time
period of their choosing by a device under the care of librarian Atoz (Ian Wolfe). By accident, Kirk is sent off to
what appears to be medieval England, where, for his
clothing and his "voices," he is jailed for witchcraft. Trying

to follow him, Spock and McCoy land in a frozen land-scape. The doctor almost dies before they are rescued by the lonely, and beautiful, Zarabeth (Mariette Hartley). Each of the officers is resuced in the proverbial nick of time, but Spock's necessary abandonment of Zarabeth makes it a less than happy ending.

Airdate: 6903.14

Episode 78: Turnabout Intruder

by Arthur Singer, from a story by Gene Roddenberry

Talk about a twist of plot—this one centers around a mind switch between Kirk and the scientist Dr. Janice Lester (Sandra Smith)! In one of his best acting efforts, Shatner manages to suggest a female mind in his male body. Un-fortunately, an anti-feminist prejudice prevails in the author's characterization: we're expected to know it's really a woman since she (it?) is emotional and vindictive. In-deed, the evil lady's motive for the switcheroo is presented as sex envy—she wanted desperately to be a man, particu-larly a man in a position of power. Captain James Kirk, for instance.

Airdate: 6906.03

**Bottom:
"The Menagerie," starring Jeffrey Hunter, is an ex-panded version of "The Cage," an early pilot. ©
Paramount Pictures Cor-poration.**

**Top:
Spock falls in love with Zarabeth, portrayed by Mariette Hartley, in "All Our Yesterdays." © Para-mount Pictures Corpo-ration.**

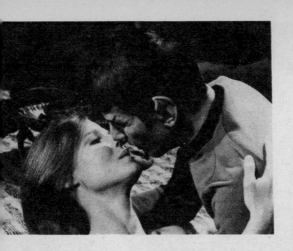

The
Animated
Star
Trek

Introduction

The disembodied voices of the **Enterprise** crew—except Walter Koenig (Ensign Chekov)— returned to the airwaves in the fall of 1972. As a network presentation, the animated **ST** lasted for most of two seasons, sixteen episodes the first season and six the second. In October 1976 Paramount Television announced that it had syndicated the animated version to twenty-five markets within just three weeks, an impressive figure.

The animated series was greeted by fans of the original show with decidedly mixed emotions. By and large, script quality on the animated episodes was high, doubtless a tribute to Dorothy Fontana (author of some of the best live-action scripts), who served as story editor and associate producer. However, many observers felt that the animation process itself was not all it might have been—particularly since animation in theory holds a natural edge over live-action in the production of special effects. Still, the addition of two crew members to the animated **Enterprise** was an interesting step in the right direction; the original series could have benefitted from their presence. Perhaps in trib-

ute to the overwhelming popularity of Mr. Spock, two new aliens joined the human folk on the bridge. The first, replacing the lamented Chekov, was Mr. Arex, a three-armed, three-legged native of the planet Edoa. The second alien, a female, was cast as Lieutenant Uhura's assistant with communications. Although humanoid, Lieutenant M'ress was very much a feline personality (her native planet: Cait).

The producers of the animated series were doubtless on the right track with these two new aliens—unfortunately, they were put to little or no use. Mr. Spock was interesting both as an alien and as a character; Lieutenant M'ress and Mr. Arex were simply aliens, interesting but essentially characterless. Of course Mr. Spock's was a bigger part—if only because of his position as second-in-command. He had more opportunity to display a rounded personality. Mr. Arex's character was limned by unending "third leg" jokes (much as Chekov's contribution was limited to the Soviets-were-first category); Lieutenant M'ress, like Lieutenant Uhura, spent too much of her time contacting

Starfleet Command, and not enough as a convincing character (and woman).

Producers, Lou Scheimer and Norm Prescott; Associate Producer, D. C. Fontana; Story Editor, D. C. Fontana; Director, Hal Sutherland. A Filmation Production, in association with Norway Productions. **Cast** (voices only): Captain James T. Kirk, William Shatner; Mr. Spock, Leonard Nimoy; Dr. McCoy, DeForest Kelley; Mr. Scott, James Doohan; Lieutenant Uhura, Nichelle Nichols; Mr. Sulu, George Takei; Nurse Chapel, Majel Barrett; Lieutenant M'ress, Majel Barrett; Lieutenant Arex, James Doohan; Ship's Computer, Majel Barrett.

First Season

Beyond the Farthest Star

by Samuel A. Peeples

Drawn to an alien starship billions of years old, the **Enterprise** doesn't know that inside the ship awaits a malevolent being seeking out a new "body." Big problems arise when the alien decides that the ideal solution is the **Enterprise**. Chilling end sequence. (Peeples wrote the pilot film "Where No Man Has Gone Before," that sold **ST** as a series.

Yesteryear

by Dorothy Fontana

Spock must return via the time portal (from "City on the Edge of Forever") to Vulcan of thirty years past to correct a distorted time line. If he fails, he will die. Charming scenes of Spock as a boy growing up make this quite possibly the animated **ST**'s best episode. Guesting, Mark

Lenard. (The story is somewhat similar to an episode of Irwin Allen's *The Time Travelers* series.)

More Tribbles, More Troubles

by David Gerrold

In this sequel to "The Trouble with Tribbles," the **Enterprise** rescues a small scout ship from a Klingon battle cruiser, only to find that they have saved Cyrano Jones—and more tribbles. This time, however, the tribbles don't multiply, they just get bigger, and bigger, and bigger. Stanley Adams guests as the voice of Jones.

The Survivor

by James Schmerer

A beauty-and-the-beast story in which a woman security officer believes that the survivor of a damaged trader ship who has just beamed aboard the **Enterprise** is her long-lost fiancé. She soon discovers that the being is not her fiancé at all—just an alien who has taken on his image. Interesting episode with some similarities to the live-action "Man Trap."

Mudd's Passion

by Steven Kandel

In Kandel's third outing with his lovable galactic con man Harcourt Fenton Mudd, Mudd is now peddling a love potion that really works. The amusing story gives excellent insights into several characters and the relationships among the **Enterprise**'s crew. Roger C. Carmel again takes on the role of Mudd.

The Magicks of Megas-Tu

by Larry Brody

The **Enterprise** is on a mission to chart the core of the galaxy and is pulled into a different time-space continuum wherein "magick" is the natural order of things. During the course of their adventure, not only are members of the **Enterprise**'s crew bound in shackles and chains, but they also meet up with the devil! Very entertaining and interesting episode. Guest voice: Ed Bishop, who played Commander Straker on *UFO*.

The Lorelei Signal

by Margaret Armen

The **Enterprise** is lured to a strange golden planet by an irresistible signal. The men all seem to be enchanted, and the women on the **Enterprise**, led by Lieutenant Uhura, must take over to save the ship. The rather ordinary script is saved by the fact that this is really the only time in **ST** that women crew members take actual command (and even here, Armen had to use a gimmick to have it happen). (Armen wrote three of the live-action scripts.)

One of Our Planets Is Missing

by Marc Daniels

Author Daniels directed fourteen live-action episodes and is considered one of television's best directors. His story here deals with a strange matter-energy cloud which is moving into our galaxy. The **Enterprise** attempts to stop it but is instead drawn into the cloud. Kirk must find a way to save his ship and crew. The quality of this well-written episode is hindered by perhaps too much of a similarity to the live-action episode "The Immunity Syndrome."

The Infinite Vulcan

by Walter Koenig

While conducting a planetary expedition, a landing party discovers a scientist who is seeking a perfect being from which he can build an army "to maintain peace in the galaxy." Who does the scientist have in mind for this perfect specimen? Spock. The fairly interesting story is marred by poor visuals. The author is the same Walter Koenig who played Ensign Chekov on seasons two and three of the original **ST**.

Time Trap

by Joyce Perry

The **Enterprise** and a Klingon battle cruiser are both drawn into the "Delta Triangle" and find out that it's a time trap from which they may never escape. Excellently conceived and directed.

The Slaver Weapon

by Larry Niven

Spock, Sulu, and Uhura are using a shuttlecraft to transport a "stasis box," a rare and valuable relic of the Slaver Empire. When they detect another such box and go to investigate, they find that they have been lured into a trap set by the savage felinoid aliens, the Kzinti. This interesting episode is highlighted by the use of two normally secondary characters in major roles. (Hugo and Nebula Award-winning author Larry Niven adapted one of his short stories as the basis for this episode.)

The Jihad

by Steven Kandel

In Kandel's second script for the animated series, Kirk and Spock are chosen to join a top secret team of aliens to accomplish a vital mission. If they do succeed, a jihad (holy war) will explode all across the galaxy. A highly enjoyable episode; one of the animated's best.

The Ambergris Element

by Marbaret Armen

Like Kandel, Margaret Armen wrote two episodes for the animated **ST**. In her second story, an **Enterprise** party takes an aquashuttle (a sort of hovercraft) down to a water planet and is attacked by a large sea creature. The aquashuttle is destroyed and both Kirk and Spock are lost, apparently drowned in the attack. When they are found, both have been transformed into fishlike beings who cannot exist out of water. A temporary solution is arrived at when McCoy builds a water tank for his captain and first officer, but all **Enterprise** crewmembers realize that Kirk will not be able to command his ship from an aquarium. How can Spock and Kirk be transformed back to normal human and Vulcan? The answer lies back on the planet in **ST**'s first look at an alien water kingdom.

Once Upon a Planet

by Lynn Janson and Chuck Menville

In this unsatisfactory adaptation of Theodore Sturgeon's live-action "Shore Leave," the recreation planet has now become a tremendously dangerous environment. Soon after an **Enterprise** landing party arrives on the planet, the amusement park's main computer system breaks down and the crew begins to be chased by fantastic creatures of their own imaginations. The poor story at least offers the wonderful singing voice of Nichelle Nichols.

The Terratin Incident

by Paul Schneider

After receiving a mysterious signal, the **Enterprise** follows the strange transmission back to its original source. Soon afterward, crew members begin to shrink. If they can't find some solution to their problem, they'll soon be too small to control the ship. (Schneider wrote two of the live-action **ST**'s most highly acclaimed episodes, "Balance of Terror" and "The Squire of Gothos.")

The Eye of the Beholder

by David Harmon

Investigating the disappearance of a science team from another ship, Kirk, Spock, and McCoy beam down to the surface of a planet and find themselves in a "zoo." The zookeepers look like giant slugs but have I.Q.'s in the thousands—and they do not intend to free their new "specimens." This delightful episode features some of the cutest of all **ST** aliens. (Harmon wrote two episodes for the live-action series, "The Deadly Years" and "A Piece of the Action," the latter co-authored with Gene L. Coon.)

Second Season

The Pirates of Orion

by Howard Weinstein

Spock has contracted a disease fatal to Vulcans, and his life depends upon the delivery of a rare drug. Complications arise when the vehicle with the shipment is forced to surrender its precious cargo to the Orions, a hostile alien race. Fairly good episode.

Albatross

by Dario Finelli

During a stop to a remote planet named Damia, the **Enterprise** crew is stunned when Dr. McCoy is arrested for the slaughter of hundreds of Damians, nineteen years before. All in all, quite interesting.

BEM

by David Gerrold

BEM is the representative of an alien race considering membership in the Federation. The **Enterprise** and her crew are among a group being tested by BEM's people as to the worthiness of the Federation—and they may fail. A good story is flawed toward its end by the use of a character who bears a disgracefully close resemblance to the Companion from the live-action "Metamorphosis."

Practical Joker

by Chuck Menville

The main computer of the **Enterprise** wreaks havoc on the

crew when electronic particles invade its circuits. The hilarious farce is highlighted by our first glimpse of the **Enterprise**'s recreation room, where the illusion of being anywhere on any world is simply a matter of programming the room's controls. (Roddenberry first created this concept when putting together the live-action series, but budget considerations intervened.)

How Sharper Than a Serpent's Tooth

by Russel Bates and David Wise

The **Enterprise** encounters a vessel that soon renders it crippled. Kulkulkan, a god that actually exists according to legend, is the "pilot" of the enemy ship and demands previously denied recognition. A rather intriguing story.

Counter-Clock Incident

by John Culver

An alien ship pulls the **Enterprise** and her crew (accompanied by Commodore Robert April, the first captain of the **Enterprise**, and his wife), into an exploding nova. There, in a reverse universe, black stars shine in the whiteness of space and people are born old and die young. Trapped, the crew begins to turn into children—losing their knowledge and space skills. The end of the episode offers a strong moral: April and his wife, who have decreased in age about forty years (to age twenty-five) decide that it is better to stay old and cherish fond memories of the past than to become young again. Very well done; the finest entry of the animated's second season.

The
Marketspace

Trekdom lives not only in the imaginations of its fans, but in a galaxy of products and merchandise. Manufac- turers, dealers and trekkers themselves have created a seemingly infinite number of items, and new fans of all ages have been attracted to the worlds of the **Enterprise**. Some products are new; others can be "stardated" to the series' first voyage into our living rooms. Some are easy to find at your local toy, hobby, department, or specialty store, or through a mail-order dealer's catalog; others are now collector's items, available only at cons.

In this section, we list **Star Trek** licensed related merchandise. National manufacturers' products are sold in department, discount, or retail specialty outlets. Any prices listed are subject to change.

Manufacturers

Aladdin Industries Products of Canada, Inc., 245 Edwards, Aurora, Ontario L46 3L4 Canada, (416) 727-1365 —Plastic lunch kits with or without bottles.

Aimo Publications, 1358 North LaBrea, Hollywood, CA 90028, (213) 469-2411—**Star Trek** theme sheet music.

A.M.T. Corporation, 1225 East Maple Road, Troy, MI 48084, (313) 589-1520—Plastic scale model kits of all inanimate (non-human) elements.

Aviva Enterprises, Inc., 111 PotreroStreet, San Francisco, CA 94103, (415) 552-6600—Banks, glass drinking glasses, bumper stickers, cloth and plastic banners, plastic and paper kites, plastic water pistols, costume jewelry, tote bags and luggage, luggage tags, mirrors, plastic and metal buttons, mugs (excluding plastic), music boxes, 3-D paper weight of the **Enterprise**, cloth patches, wall plaques, plastic and paper playing cards, ladies' scarves, stained-glass decorative window ornaments and stained glass kits, stationery supplies, plastic and wooden yo-yos, portable trays and television trays, plastic party goods, night lights, bulletin boards, 3-D stickers, glossy color photographs, electric and non-electric toothbrushed, medical supplies, color-your-own poster kit, cardboard jigsaw puzzles, stand-up cardboard character cutouts, non-die-cast painted figurines, walkers, belt buckles.

Azrak-Hamway International, Inc., 1107 Broadway, New York, NY 10010, (212) 675-3427—Bagatelle, Bop Bags, U-Fly-It **Enterprise**.

Bally Manufacturing Corporation, 2640 Belmont Avenue, Chicago, IL, (312) 267-6060—Coin-operated pinball machine.

Milton Bradley Company, 1500 Main Street, Springfield, MA 01101, (413) 525-6400—Electronic and non-electronic games, Porta-Vee, **Enterprise**, Phaser, Tricorder, Cast-N'-Paint sculptured figures with paint, 3-D foam-core poster art board, vinyl window forms, puzzles.

Bradley Time, 1115 Broadway, New York, NY 10010, (212) 243-0200—Wristwatches, clocks.

Coleco Industries, 200 Fifth Avenue, New York, NY 10010—Programmed computer game, non-coin-operated pinball machine.

Deka Plastic, 914 Westfield Avenue, Elizabeth, NJ 07208, (201) 351-0900—Plastic dinnerware.

Futorian Corporation, 666 Lakeshore Drive, Chicago, IL 60611, (312) 642-5604—Bead-filled furniture.

GAF Corporation, 150 West 51st Street, New York, NY 10020, (212) 582-7600—Color slide reels.

Glen Shoe Company, Inc., 47 West 34th Street, New York, NY 10001, (212) 239-6740—Men's, women's, and children's footwear.

Don Halvorsen-Scaniens Sweets Pty. Ltd., 99 Shepherd Street, Chippendale, N.S.W. 2008, Australia—Swap cards with confectionary /bubble gum.

Heritage Models, 9840 Monroe Drive, Building 106, Dallas, TX 75220, (214) 351-3708—Non-articulate centrifugal (metal) figures.

Ideal Toy Corporation, 184-10 Jamaica Avenue, Hollis, NY 11423, (212) 454-5000—Silent film cartridge.

Lee Company, Empire State Building, New York, NY 10001, (212) 244-4440—Belts (plastic, synthetic, leather).

E. Martinoni Company, 543 Forbes Boulevard, South San Francisco, CA 94080, (415) 873-3000—Liquor bottle in shape of Mr. Spock.

Meccano, Ltd., c /o Airfix Industries, Ltd., 17 Old Court Place, London W8 4QF, England—Die-cast Klingon and **Enterprise** models.

Mego Corporation, 206 Fifth Avenue, New York, NY 10010, (212) 689-8600—Pre-assembled puppets, articulated figures, electronic target games, walkie-talkies, transistor radios.

Open Door Enterprises, Inc., 1201 Comstock Street, Santa Clara, CA, (408) 985-2660—String art kit.

Pajama Corporation of America, 350 Fifth Avenue, New York, NY, (212) 736-2940—Men's, boys', infants' woven knit pajamas and robes.

Edizione Panini Spa, Viale Emilio Po n. 380, 41100 Moden, Italy. Tel. U.S.: (415) 982-7557—Sticker box.

Peter Pan Industries, 145 Kormorn Street, Newark, NJ 07105, (201) 344-4214—Record and book sets, long-playing record albums.

Phoenix Candy Company, 151-65 35th Street, Brooklyn, NY 11232, (212) 768-7986—Cardboard containers, candy, prizes.

Pocket Books, 1230 Avenue of the Americas, New York, NY 10020, (212) 246-2121—Various publications.

Random House, 201 East 50th Street, New York, NY 10020, (212) 751-2600—Pop-up books for children.

Tam O'Shanter Textiles Ltd., 9250 Park Avenue, Montreal, Quebec, Canada H2N 2A1, (514) 381-8641—T-shirts and sweatshirts.

Topps Chewing Gum, Inc., 254 26th Street, Brooklyn, NY 11232, (212) 768-8900—Chewing gum, bubble gum, candy with or without picture trading cards, stickers, rub-on tattoos and /or containers, posters.

Preceding page:
Azrak-Hamway International, Inc., has a Phaser Saucer Gun with three multi-colored flying saucers in safe and durable materials.

Left:
Editor Gerry Turnbull has always enjoyed shopping, especially for ST merchandise. Photo: Neil Appelbaum.

Bottom:
The GAF View-Master stereo packets offer hours of three-dimensional viewing entertainment.

VIEW-MASTER 21 Stereo Pictures

The Bookcase

A little more to the left...that's good...now scratch.

Trek or Treat,
from Ballantine
Books, has some-
thing for everyone.

In between watching TV reruns and reading zines, fans turn to the ever-growing number of books to satisfy their **Star Trek** hunger. Have you missed any on the list below? **This listing is comprehensive but not necessarily complete; new books appear on the market frequently. Although we have checked the facts carefully wherever possible, we cannot be responsible for any inaccuracies or changes that may occur.**

I Am Not Spock, by Leonard Nimoy, Celestial Arts, 1976. $4.95.
Where Spock ends and the real Leonard Nimoy begins—by the one who knows best, a charming autobiography.

Letters to Star Trek, edited by Susan Sackett, Ballantine Books, January 1977. $1.95.
The best of the tons of letters sent to the **ST** staff and stars, and their answers. Introduction by Gene Roddenberry, new photos.

The Making of Star Trek by Stephen E. Whitfield and Gene Roddenberry, Ballantine Books. $1.95.
Everything you always wanted to know about the series—how, when, where **Star Trek** was born, grew—and was born again!

Six Science Fiction Plays, Roger Elwood, Editor, Pocket Books, 1976. $1.95.
Includes one of the outstanding **Star Trek** episodes, Harlan Ellison's original screenplay for his "City on the Edge of Forever," Hugo Award winner.

Spock, Messiah! by Theodore R. Cogswell and Charles A. Spano, Jr., Bantam Books, September 1976. $1.75.
A chiller-thriller novel of adventure.

Spock Must Die! by James Blish, Bantam Books, 1979. $1.25
The master science-fiction writer's original novel, based on the Spock character.

It goes well with your high heels.

Star Fleet Technical Manual, designed by Franz Joseph,
Ballantine Books, 1975. $6.95.
Complete guidebook to the **Enterprise** and the United
Federation of Planets. Includes the Articles of Federation,
all the insignia of the armed forces of the Federation, de-
tailed descriptions of the ships in the fleet, etc. Technical
drawings accompany text.

Star Trek series, adaptations of the TV episodes in short-
story form. Sold in single copies and boxed sets of six.

Star Trek 1 by James Blish, Bantam Books. $1.25.
Adaptations of: "Charlie's Law," "Dagger of the Mind,"
"The Unreal McCoy," "Balance of Terror," "The Naked
Time," "Miri," "The Conscience of the King."

Star Trek 2 by James Blish, Bantam Books. $1.25.
Adaptations of: "Arena," "A Taste of Armageddon,"
"Tomorrow Is Yesterday," "Errand of Mercy," "Court
Martial," "Operation—Annihilate!" "The City on the Edge
of Forever," * "Space Seed."

Star Trek 3 by James Blish, Bantam Books. $1.25.
Adaptations of: "The Trouble with Tribbles," "The Last
Gunfight," "The Doomsday Machine," "Assignment:
Earth," "Mirror, Mirror," "Friday's Child," "Amok Time."

Star Trek 4 by James Blish, Bantam Books. $1.25.
Adaptations of: "All Our Yesterdays," "The Devil in the
Dark," "Journey to Babel," "The Menagerie," * * "The En-
terprise Incident," "A Piece of the Action."

Star Trek 5 by James Blish, Bantam Books. $1.25.
Adaptations of: "Whom the Gods Destroy," "The Tholian
Web," "Let That Be Your Last Battlefield," "This Side of
Paradise," "Turnabout Intruder," "Requiem for
Methuselah," "This Way to Eden."

*Winner, International Hugo Award for Best Dramatic
Presentation of the year. Also voted best TV script of the
year by the TV writers.
* *Winner, Hugo Award for Best Dramatic Presentation of
the year.

Star Trek 6 by James Blish, Bantam Books. $1.25.
Adaptations of: "The Savage Curtain," "The Lights of
Zetar," "The Apple," "By Any Other Name," "The Cloud
Minders," "The Mark of Gideon."

Star Trek 7 by James Blish, Bantam Books. $1.25.
Adaptations of: "Who Mourns for Adonis?," "The Change-
ling," "The Paradise Syndrome," "Metamorphosis," "The
Deadly Years," "Elaan of Troyius."

Star Trek 8 by James Blish, Bantam Books. $1.25.
Adaptations of: "Spock's Brain," "The Enemy Within,"
"Catspaw," "Where No Man Has Gone Before," "Wolf in
the Fold," "For the World Is Hollow and I Have Touched
the Sky."

Star Trek 9 by James Blish, Bantam Books. $1.25.
Adaptations of: "Return to Tomorrow," "The Ultimate
Computer," "That Which Survives," "Obsession," "The
Return of the Archons," "The Immunity Syndrome."

Star Trek 10 by James Blish, Bantam Books. $1.25.
Adaptations of: "The Alternative Factor," "The Empath,"
"The Galileo Seven," "Is There in Truth No Beauty?" "A
Private Little War," "The Omega Glory."

Star Trek 11 by James Blish, Bantam Books. $1.25.
Adaptations of: "What Are Little Girls Made Of?" "The
Squire of Gothos," "The Wind of an Eye," "Bread and
Circuses," "Day of the Dove," "Plato's Stepchildren."

Star Trek Blueprints by Franz J. Schnaubelt, Ballantine
Books, 1975. $5.00.
Starship blueprint designs in detail, exterior and interior
views—sick bay, bridge, Spock's science lab, every level
of the **Enterprise**, etc., in exact scale.

Star Trek Concordance by Bjo Trimble, Ballantine Books. $5.95.
Complete encyclopedia and cross-reference of people, places and things in Trekdom, with drawings and photos.

Star Trek Lives by Jacqueline Lichtenberg, Sondra Marshak and Joan Winston, Bantam Books, July 1975. $1.95.
An in-depth examination of the creators, crew, fans, conventions and stars of **Star Trek**.

Star Trek Log One through **Nine**, by Alan Dean Foster, Ballantine Books. $1.50 each.

Star Trek Log series, adaptations of the TV animated episodes in story form. Sold in single copies and boxed sets of four.

The Star Trek Reader by James Blish, E. P. Dutton & Co., October 1976. $8.95.
Adaptations of twenty-one **Star Trek** TV scripts in a hard-cover edition.

Star Trek—The New Voyages, Myrna Culbreath and Sondra Marshak, Bantam Books, 1976. $1.75.
New, original adventures—exciting new stories.

The Trouble with Tribbles by David Gerrold, Ballantine Books, October, 1976. $1.95.
The ups and downs and ins and outs of the making of the very popular Tribbles episode.

Will I Think of You? by Leonard Nimoy, Celestial Arts. $3.95.
Nimoy's deeply emotional love poem. His word pictures are as beautiful as his photography.

The World of Star Trek by David Gerrold, Ballantine Books, 1973. $1.95.
A fascinating inside view of the **Trek** saga, its past, present and future. Makes you feel like part of the crew.

Trek or Treat by Eleanor Ehrhardt & Terry Flanagan, Ballantine Books, 1977. $2.95.
Picture book of the **Trek** stars with space balloon captions that are as amusing as blooper reels.

You and I by Leonard Nimoy, Celestial Arts. $3.95.
Nimoy's superb photographs and poetry, beautifully presented.

Children's Books

Action Toy Book, designed by James Razzi, Random House, 1976. $2.95.
Toys are punched out, assembled, then made to move. Includes a ray gun, Klingon cruiser, tricorder, phaser, universal translator, communicator, **Enterprise**, and Vulcan ears.

Puzzle Manual by James Razzi, Bantam Books, 1976. $5.95.
Includes mazes, puzzles, and trivia. Older Trekkies can enjoy it too, especially the trivia.

New and Upcoming Children's Books

Giant in the Universe, Random House (a pop-up book)

Trillions of Trilligs, Random House (a pop-up book)

The Truth Machine, a Random House Juvenile Book (story book)

Prisoner of Vega, a Random House Juvenile Book (story book)

Top:
Peter Pan Industries offers ST stories on records with exciting illustrated covers and worthwhile listening pleasure.

Left:
This Action Toy Book from Random House contains eight cut-out toys in brightly colored laminated cardboard.

The Future
Voyages

STAR TREK—THE MOTION PICTURE SET FOR BIG SCREEN! The news, released in 1976, that Paramount planned to produce a feature film reuniting as many of the crew of the **Enterprise** as possible was met with cheers from **ST** fans, and with feelings of victory as well. Ever since the demise of the series, a barrage of letters and petitions has been pounding the offices of network and studio executives, the messages all variants on the theme summed up most succinctly in a slogan seen on buttons and bumper stickers: BRING BACK **STAR TREK!**

Star Trek, the forerunner of *Star Wars, Close Encounters of the Third Kind* and *Battlestar Galactica* can only be met with like success as Paramount, in a move unprecedented in the annals of film distribution, billed **Star Trek—The Motion Picture** for Christmas 1979 release over a year before it will reach the screen. This of course was done in an effort to secure prime theaters for the most competitive of film seasons.

Several times prior to the Paramount announcement, rumors had been started and spread. The show, fans told

one another, was set for a major return. And always the rumors turned out to be founded more in wishful thinking than in substantive fact. This time, however, it's different. As we go to press, many members of the original starship crew have been signed for at least one more trek (this time on the big screen) and possibly two! Although there were some major delays involving the contractual demands of lead players and the script itself has gone through several drafts and major revisions, production plans appear to have been finalized at last. The major delay was attributed to the adding of technical achievements first utilized in *Star Wars*.

The **ST** movie is shrouded in secrecy, with a closed set and closed mouths. Fans have waited so long to see their dream come true that it is only understandable that the studio wants to capitalize on the full impact of surprise as to the latest "mission" of the **Enterprise**.

Where will **ST** go from the big screen? Industry insiders hint that if the movie is successful, as it is sure to be, more features will be made—not only for theatrical release, but

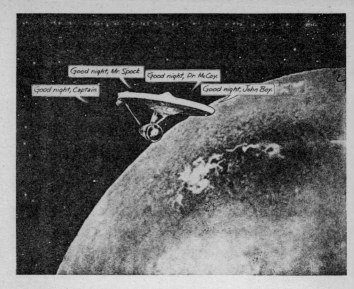

perhaps new movies for television as well. The special effects that characterized the TV series won praise and admiration from professionals and the public alike. With more time, a bigger budget, and some of the recent new frontiers crossed in the studio special effects field, the new **ST** promises to be even more exciting. With the phenomenal success of *Battlestar Galactica* there seems to be no reason why a successful series should not be made from the movie.

What about the hundreds of thousands of letters that have poured into TV station and network offices? While they haven't as yet brought the show back on a weekly basis, they've certainly stimulated production of the new movie and the syndication of the original series, and helped to create the books, records, games, greeting cards, puzzles, toys, and novelty items.

The spirit of those letters has led to clubs and fan organizations, to friendships and new acquaintances, and to ever broadening horizons of imagination for the millions for whom **STAR TREK** LIVES!